ALL ABOUT ISLAM

Knowing More About Islam

Arham Khaliq Khan

Mirza Areeb Beg

Made with ❤ on the Notion Press Platform

www.notionpress.com

GUIDE US ALONG THE STRAIGHT PATH

[Quran 1: 6]

Contents

A) *Common questions in and about Islam.*

B) *Ending the debate of prophet Muhammad's (ﷺ) marriage with Hazrat Aishah (RA) and his multiple marriages*

C)*Famous personalities about Islam and its Messenger*

D)*Some lessons from the Quran*

E)*99 Names of Allah*

Preface

The book **ALL ABOUT ISLAM** came into being with the idea to show what Islam is and what Islam really looks like.

With All praises and victories to *ALLAH* and with the help of him we the authors of the book ARHAM And AREEB came up with an idea to bring near the truth by showing you the utmost beauty of him (ALLAH) his last messenger *Prophet Muhammad* () and the religion *ISLAM* in the most appealing way we can.

This book is not only for the one who has become wicked and the one who is righteous. This book also belongs to all those non-Muslims who want to get aware of the real image of Islam and the beauty of it in a perceptive manner.

This book is mainly written with the help of *Quran*, teachings of Prophet Muhammad (ﷺ) and by the will of ALLAH

✯✯✯

Acknowledgments

Special thanks to Allah the Guide because of his will, his final revelation and the teachings of the last Prophet Muhammad (ﷺ), we were able to write the book you read. Without him we are nothing.

All glory and victory belong to him,

and what he wills shall be ours.

Second, we thank Dr Mustafa Khattab through his translation of the Quran named (The Clear Quran) the poems were written leaving only three that are Palestine, Thoughts and Introductory Poem. And with the help various web pages and sites that helped us a lot which are as follows: -

- https://www.iium.edu.my/deed/articles/thelastsermon.html
- https://sunnah.com/
- and many more…

We surely apologize to any site we forgot and missed to mention here, and we truly thank all sites with our heart.

Finally, we would like to thank all the Islamic Scholars like Dr Zakir Naik, Dr Israr Ahmad, Mufti Menk, Tariq Jameel and many more.

★★★

INTRODUCTORY

All About Islam aims to give a brief sketch or explanation of Islam or some of the important topics that come under this religion or some that moves around it.

It might be quite short but relevant to make you nearer to the truth about Islamic ideology. Like any human being who has sinned a lot and has gone far astray. ALLAH forgives each one of those who repent with heart and come back to him.

No matter how far you have gone from Allah it just takes a single step to come under his mercy again and remember ALLAH is the most forgiving, most merciful.

This Book is mostly written with the help of the Quran and sayings of the prophet Muhammad (ﷺ) (Hadees) and both doesn't force you to be a Muslim but teaches you how to become a better human being and make the world or surroundings a better place. The purpose of this book is also the same and to teach you what Islam really looks like and what it is. No one has the right to act or to force somebody to be someone, and anyone can do anything what he wants (Anything good) that's what we all call freedom. But everyone has the right to speak; that's what we all call freedom of speech. And in fact, *it is stated in the Quran (2:256) that let there be no compulsion in the religion, for the truth stands out clearly from falsehood. (in brief) The verse clearly prohibits forced conversion.*

What's the content inside?

Islamic ideology illustrated in it
Impervious impenetrable info included
Indeed, in-depth ideas illuminated
Indispensable indisputable info in it

Straight standard steadied
Sagacious sapiently seriesed
Spared suffice studied
Sources Splendidly schemed

Laborious lavish logical
Lofted literature lovable
Lucid lessons learnable
Limpid lenient legible

About Above All
Altogether assembled aright
Appealing attentive actual
And absolute alright

Muhammad (ﷺ) marvelous message
Majesty mercy mentioned
Moreover, magnetic manner
Much More Most

Would it be helpful?

Yes, for sure, it will be helpful for all. By making the righteous closer and showing the wicked the right way. It will help the one who is just a step behind and the one who is far away. And for the non-Muslims to know the truth about Islam and understand it in an easier way than ever to be.

UNIT I: GOD

To be closer you shall believe,
and to believe
There must be someone to believe in.

But this book isn't named CLOSER TO ALLAH. It is named ALL ABOUT ISLAM which teaches About Allah, Islam and its beauty. No creation can be created without a creator. whether it's the mobile you use, or a chair on which you use your mobile while sitting on, or the wood from which the chair was made and the carpenter who extracted the wood from the tree to create that chair, but this cycle should come to an end. And where should it end? The Perfect and the most Logical answer we all get is: -

GOD

to where all the things end,
From where all the things start.

With this concept the book begins with the chapter *ALLAH* and ends with chapter *ALLAH'S MERCY* and a last chapter is named as thoughts which is like a conclusion to the book.

I

GOD

No vision can grasp Him, but His grasp is over all vision. He is above all comprehension yet is acquainted with all things.

(Quran 6:103)

Everything that we see around is created by someone, may it be houses, roads, TV's or the Book/Phone in your hands right now. Everything that exists, exists through someone who made it to exist. Everything designed has a designer, even a piece of paper is created by someone but on contrary some people think that the entire universe, which is expanding and moving in a perfect rhythm and with stability has been created by a blast. No, it is not! There must be someone who created all that we see, there must be someone who made us so perfectly despite being so complex. And yes, there is someone who made us and that is God. If you show someone an RC Car and ask them who made them, they will say that it is made by an engineer/human but if you ask them who made you the way you are? Despite being so much more complex than a RC car, some of the people would completely black out or just give a ridiculous explanation of how the life started from the Big Bang.

The concept of believing in god can be different, you may believe in a single God, a single God with various other forms or Many Gods. Believing in many gods is known as Polytheism and the polytheist people believe that the universe is not controlled by a single Divine God but rather by many gods. They seek refuge not from one alone Divine God but from different other beings. Idolatry can be understood as an example for Polytheism, people worship many idols and ask from them for help. There are many religions which are based on Polytheism, like one of the major religion Hinduism, but what if I tell you that Hinduism is also concentrated to single God. The main scriptures of Hinduism like the Upanishads and Vedas mention that there is only one Divine being which further become many, or from which further formed different deities (Devtas) [**Chandogya Upanishad 6:2:1** *(sadeva somyedamagra āsīdekamevādvitīyam | taddhaika āhurasadevedamagra āsīdekamevādvitīyaṃ tasmādasataḥ sajjāyata) Somya, before this world was manifest there was only existence, one without a second. On this subject, some maintain that before this world was manifest there was only non-existence, one without a second. Out of that non-existence, existence emerged.]*, The main Hindu philosophy includes the existence of the Paramatma (The supreme Self). The core concept of Christianity and Judaism is also Monotheist. Islam is also a Monotheist faith, and Muslims believe in the one and only god Allah. You might have understood by now that all these major religions have the same exact concept of one single God, but they just got misguided and started practicing something like Polytheism. But why is Polytheism wrong? It is simple! If you created something and people started to associate different partners with you, would you like it? Absolutely Not. Till now you must have understood that the universe is being controlled by God. But you might be wondering, why can't be there multiple gods? So, the answer to this can be easy if you try to understand it in some local context. Like can you imagine a country which is ruled by two rulers at once, or a car with more than one driver? I suppose not and this is the answer to your question. There can't be more than a single Divine God, and Allah says in the Qur'an that if there were more than two gods then there would have been corruption both in the heavens and the earth (Qur'an 21:22).

'O believers! ˈ Do not insult what they invoke besides Allah, or they will insult Allah spitefully out of ignorance. This is how We have made each people's deeds appealing to them. Then to their Lord is their return, and He will inform them of what they used to do.

(Qur'an 6:108)

ALLAH

Who is Allah? Allah is the one God whom the Muslims believe in. He is the Almighty, the All Knower, The Rabb of the Alamin, the creator of the heavens and the earth, the creator of the entire Universe. He is the Lord of Abraham, Isaac, Jacob, Moses, Jesus as well as the Lord of Prophet Muhammad (ﷺ). He is the owner of the divine wisdom and knows what is unknown, he is the doer of the impossible, he is the only God in which the Muslims believe and is the master of the mankind. Whenever we think we are alone and no one is seeing us, remember there is Allah under whose vision is everything. Whenever we are facing a problem, it is Allah who is testing us through those problems and surely with hardships there is ease. Allah does not need anyone or anything, it is just us who need Allah. Allah is the one who created us and he is the one who can destroy us in an instance like the people of Lut (Lot) and the people of Nuh (Noah). Now for the most important part is how can we connect with Allah. So, the first step which brings us closer to Allah, we have already taken it by simply just reading this book and it is to know about Allah. We can only connect with Allah if we know who Allah is and what Allah can do. Another question might also come to you which is Where is Allah? As per many scholars Allah is not bound to any place, he is present wherever he wants to be (however it befits his glory) and from some evidence, it is said that Allah is above the heavens, over his throne (however it befits his glory), Allah knows best. Why does Allah not show himself? This can be answered through the Qur'an, it is stated in the Qur'an that, When Moses came at the appointed time and his Lord spoke to him, he asked, "My Lord! Reveal Yourself to me so I may see You." Allah answered, "You cannot see Me! But look at the mountain. If it remains firm in its place, only then will you see Me." When his Lord appeared to the mountain, He levelled it to dust, and Moses collapsed unconscious. When he recovered, he cried, "Glory be to You! I turn to You in repentance, and I am the first of the believers."

Many people believe that the Qur'an is written by or is the word of Prophet Muhammad (ﷺ), but it is completely wrong, The Qur'an is the word of Allah, it was revealed to prophet Muhammad (ﷺ) through Angel Gabriel over a period of 23 years, The Prophet recited the Qur'an and the scribes wrote it down. And to prove that the Qur'an is the word of God, it has many scientific miracles stated in it which at that time were unknown like the formation of humans from gametes and formation and development of foetus, which an ordinary man (Prophet Muhammad (ﷺ) as seen by non-Muslims) wouldn't have known in a deserted country where there was no development (even 1400 years ago). We all know that travelling to space was not possible 1400 years ago, so there would be no chance that Prophet Muhammad (ﷺ) knew about the movement of the earth (Rotation of the Earth) but guess what Qur'an also speaks about the movement of the earth in Surah Naml verse number 88. There are more such proves which we will further discuss in a separate chapter but all these statements in the Qur'an prove that the Qur'an is not the word of Prophet Muhammad (ﷺ) but rather the word of someone more Superior.

This chapter is not presented to you to force you to believe in Allah it is just presented to you to believe that there is a god, not many but one, even different religions believe in monotheism, but they just got separated on some disputes. So if you want to know about the real God you have to study about it, you have to know who is a god and the claims of different religions for God, then only you can get to know who is God and for you to know this, you have to study different religions unbiasedly and understand them, only then you can come to know the TRUTH.

Aisha said, "If anyone tells you that Muhammad has seen his Lord, he is a liar, for Allah says: 'No vision can grasp Him.' (6.103) And if anyone tells you that Muhammad has seen the Unseen, he is a liar, for Allah says: "None has the knowledge of the Unseen but Allah."

(Sahih Bukhari 7380)

Allah is the creator of Heavens and earth
To be worshiped he has the worth
He knows the past and what yet to come
He is the one who provide you with wisdom

When Allah wills something to create
Then He says "be and it is"
He requires neither a parent, child or associate
He is the one who brings sadness and bliss

Allah is aware of whatever you do
Whether you are Christian, Muslim or Jew
He is the knower of the unseen
The earth, heaven & what lies between

Allah subjectected the sun and the moon
each orbiting for an appointed term
He has placed into the earth, mountains
so, it (earth) does not shake with us and stays firm

Allah created the heavens and the earth
and the alternation of the day and night
He is the one who made the sun a radiant source
And the moon a reflected light

With precisely ordained phases so you may know
the numbers of years and calculate the time
And he is the one who sends down rain from the sky
Causing all kinds of plants on earth to grow

With it he produces various crops
And created humans from sperm drops
Also landmarks and stars from people find their way
It is upon God 'Alone' to 'clearly' show you the straight
way

From cattle's bellies, between blood and digested food

he gives pure milk pleasant to drink
He Sent down the rain from the sky bringing forth
gardens and grains for harvest with clustered fruit

And with rain we revive the lifeless land
Surely in this are the signs for the people who
understand
By his will existence and time came into effect
Surely in this are the signs for the people who reflect

Allah is the one who made the stars
As your guide through your darkness of land and sea [All Above]

All the signs are in the Quran throughout
How far from truth can someone then deluded be

Reference...

All Above) All signs are mentioned are from the Quran which are- **Quran** 2:164, 3:190, 6:95-99, 7:56-58, 10:5-6, 13:2-4, 16:3-13,16:65-69, 16:79, 23:27-30, 23:115, 27:60-65, 29:44, 30:8, 44:38-39, 75:36 etc. There are still many signs not mentioned above the poem, some of them are formation and developmental phases of an embryo 22:5, 23:12-14, foetus in three layers of darkness 39:6: earth's rotation 27: 88, the big bang 21:30, black holes 81: 15-16 and many more. Although the Quran isn't the book of science but the book of signs, wisdom, way of life etc. there are still various scientific references mentioned above some which came to be known only in the last two centuries, but the Quran has already been revealed 1400 years ago.

UNIT II: Previous Scriptures and Prophets

Allah revealed various **scriptures** to prophets before revealing the final revelation, but they all were distorted, divided, wrongly translated, changed according to wish and misinterpreted by the disbelievers and they used to believe in some parts of it and not in others which were against them.

Prophet Muhammad (ﷺ) wasn't the only prophet/messenger of Allah many came before him. The first one is prophet Adam and the last is the seal of prophets which is prophet Muhammad (ﷺ). There were many prophets that came in between but only twenty five are mentioned in the Quran which by order are Prophet Adam , Idris , Nuh , Hud , Saleh , **Ibrahim(Abraham)** , Lut , Ismail , Ishaq ,Yaqub ,Yusuf , Shuaib , Ayyub , Dhulkifl, **Musa(Moses)** , Dawud , Sulayman , Ilyas , Alyasa , Yunus , Zakariya , Yahaya , **Isa(Jesus)** and at last Prophet Muhammad (ﷺ) , all of them spread the same message monotheism , to do good and to be good .Islam didn't start 1400 years ago . It started with Prophet Adam the first human being and the Kaaba was built by the prophet Ibrahim 5000 years ago not by prophet Muhammad (ﷺ). Both prophet Adam and Ibrahim are believed by all Abrahamic religions (Judaism, Christianity, and Islam). Out of twenty-five only the highlighted three are discussed here because of their major significance and impact.

II

PREVIOUS SCRIPTURES

They, the people of the Scriptures, divided this Scripture into parts, believing in some portions of it and disbelieving the others.

(Sahih al-Bukhari 3945)

To study about anything, we need some books or scriptures. Every study done is written down as a book for the future generation to learn about it, may it be sciences of the world or the history of the ancient times. Same goes for religion. To spread the teachings of a religion, scriptures are written, people read these scriptures to learn about their religion or to learn about other religions. In Islam some prophets were sent with scriptures, like Jesus with his Gospel (Injeel), Moses with his Torah (Torat) and David with his Psalms (Zabur). Quran is also the scripture of God and was sent down to Prophet Muhammad (ﷺ) for the entire mankind and the Qur'an is protected by the Almighty and no one can alter the verses of it unlike the verses from the gospels or Torah. The previous scriptures were sent down to the specific Ummah of some prophets unlike the Qur'an which is revealed to guide the entire mankind. It is also mentioned in the Qur'an that the Bani Israel used to misinterpret or change the verses from the previous scriptures and till now some of the verses of the Bible are altered. You may wonder that if the previous scriptures were the teachings of God for the people like the

Qur'an, then why not Allah sent just one Scripture for guiding the people? So, we must know that although the scriptures were written by the one and only god Allah, they all contained different guidance and teachings because the people at the times of different prophets were indulged in different wrong deeds. So, to guide the misguided people at different times different scriptures were revealed.

Scriptures were sent down by Allah to different prophets as guidance for the people but most of them were altered by the wicked and were misused by the wicked people to misguide others. Now the main question is Why did Allah NOT preserve the Previous Scriptures like The Qur'an?

Here you are! You disputed about what you have ˹little˺ knowledge of, but why do you now argue about what you have no knowledge of? Allah knows and you do not know.

(Quran 3:36)

Allah has too sent scriptures before
like the Torah, psalms Gospel and the Abraham scrolls
which got miss altered by the wicked souls
and now they aren't authentic anymore

Allah gave psalms to Prophet David (Dawud) as a
scripture revealed after the prophet of jews[1]
and even revealed a scripture to Prophet Abraham
before
Yet they deny the signs and yet they ignore

Allah gave Torah to Prophet Moses (Musa)
and gave Gospel to people of Jesus (Isa)
it wasn't God, they created monasticism by themselves
it wasn't God it was they who let their faith delves

★★★

III

PREVIOUS PROPHETS

Allah's Messenger (ﷺ) said, "My similitude in comparison with the other prophets before me, is that of a man who has built a house nicely and beautifully, except for a place of one brick in a corner. The people go about it and wonder at its beauty but say: 'Would that this brick be put in its place!' So I am that brick, and I am the last of the Prophets."

(Sahih Al-Bukhari 3535)

Prophet Ibrahim (Abraham)

Nowadays we flex our friends, we have friends who are businessmen, politicians, kings, and many more powerful people. We feel that we have friendship with many great people but what about a man who is not just a friend of people, businessmen, traders and many great people but rather a friend with the creator of the entire universe, the creator of mankind. A man who is a friend of the Almighty Allah. Yes, we are talking about the father of prophets, the friend of Allah, Ibrahim Khalilullah AS.

Ibrahim AS is one of the few prophets mentioned in the Quran and is one of the most frequently mentioned prophets. He is known as the father of prophets because the Prophets who came after him were all descendants of him whether it be Isa ibn Maryam AS (Jesus) or Muhammad (ﷺ). He is an important figure not only in Islam but also in Christianity and Judaism, but the difference is the perspective, the difference is of how they portray him, but one thing is common that they all believe that he prayed to One and only one God. From his life there are many lessons to learn, not only about Islamic Monotheism but also about many other important aspects of life. He has been through many great difficulties and tests, but these were not as great as his faith in Allah. Allah blessed him, then tested him by almost taking that blessing away from him. What we do in such situations, sadly we stop trusting in Allah and take his tests as a burden on our souls, but this was not the case of many prophets, especially Ibrahim AS. Let us look onto some of the tests, miracles and lessons from the life of Khalilullah.

In the era of Prophet Ibrahim, Idol worshiping was thriving. People of Babylon were indulged in pleasing the false gods, even the father of Prophet Ibrahim was an Idol Worshipper. His father was an idol sculptor and Ibrahim AS grew around these people who believed in the false god, despite being in the wrong company. Ibrahim AS wasn't influenced by this bad company because the heart which is purified by the Almighty can never be doomed by humans. He tried to explain to people that these statues cannot protect or help them, but the people were so indulged in the practices of their ancestors that they didn't even try to understand Ibrahim's guidance. One day prophet Ibrahim broke all the idols and when the people saw the broken idols they were very angry and wanted to know about the person who broke those statues, Ibrahim AS came up and confessed that he broke the idols and said to them that the statues that can't even protect themselves from a human, can by what means save them from much bigger problems. Due to prophet Ibrahim's regular refusal of idolatry, he was taken to king's court (Nimrod/Namroud's court). Both had a debate on the idea of God and when Nimrod got annoyed by prophet Ibrahim AS, he ordered him to be thrown in the fire. Prophet Ibrahim was thrown in the fire, but the fire couldn't harm Ibrahim AS because the fire, whose nature is to burn things, has been ordered to cool down by its creator. The fire, which is able to destroy a whole building, a colony and even a whole forest was not able to even put a scratch on a single person, because that person was not a regular man, he was man of faith, a man favored by God, a man who guided pagans on the land of paganism, indeed he was Khalilullah. This story is no less than a miracle yet understandable as it's not only believed in Islam but also in Christianity and Judaism but what makes the three religions different and makes Islam the right one? We will get our answers through the life of other prophets as we will move further but first let us know about a great test of Ibrahim AS which makes him a prime example of complete submission to the will of Allah.

By the time of his 80's, Ibrahim AS had no child and was very sad because of it. After continuous prayers to the Almighty, he was blessed with a boy who later became a prophet, he was Ismail AS. When Ismail AS grew up, prophet Ibrahim AS saw a dream in which Allah ordered him to slaughter his son (Ismail AS) for the sake of Allah. Now imagine you and we get anything after continuous struggles and prayer and then we are ordered to leave that thing, would we be able to do that? I suppose many of us won't. But Ibrahim AS even agreed to slaughter his own child, why? Because it was the order from his creator, it was the order from his lord, and this is what makes him Khalilullah. He told Ismail AS about his dream and Ismail AS also being a true believer of Allah agreed to be sacrificed for the will of Allah. He then took Ismail AS to a cliff and set up to sacrifice him, he put a strap on his eyes to not be able to look in the eyes of his only beloved son. As he began to sacrifice his son, by the will of Allah, a lamb came there, and the lamb was sacrificed. But why did that happen? Because Allah did not want the sacrifice from Ibrahim, but he rather wanted the faith of Ibrahim AS. Allah did not want blood from Ibrahim AS, but he wanted his intentions, he wanted to check the faith of Ibrahim. This is what makes Ibrahim AS a great example of sacrifice as well, this test shows that a true believer would sacrifice anything beloved to him for the sake of Allah. This incident is also the reason why Muslims from all over the world celebrate Eid ul Adha every year.

Now, what are the lessons that we should take from the life of Prophet Ibrahim's life?

A prophet who was a nation by himself
a man called as the father of the prophets
a man known as the friend of Almighty
among all major religions[2] he is the most respected to be
a prophet who comes under the top five[3]
the ancestor from whom except one other's have derive

Prophet who raised foundation of the Kaaba with his son[4]
and called his people to worship the one true god
he spread message to many but to believe there was only one[5]
a prophet who asked for the messenger[6] from the lord
he was neither a Jew nor a Christian
but the one submitted his full will to God

Prophet Musa (Moses)

In today's world, everything is about networking, everything is about how many powerful people are in connection with us. We speak to different people, but this prophet didn't just speak to normal people just like us, but he was also able to directly communicate with the creator of the world, the Almighty Allah. He was Prophet Musa or commonly known as Moses in Christianity and Judaism. Prophet Musa is the most mentioned Prophet in the Qur'an and is among the five major prophets. Prophet Musa was a descendant of Ibrahim AS and has a great role in Judaism also, which we will understand through a story of a cruel pharaoh and prophet Musa. Also, we need to know that Prophet Musa was a prophet sent for Bani Israel (Today mainly Jews).

Unlike Prophet Ibrahim, Prophet Musa was born in the family of believers, his mother was a pious woman. When prophet Musa was born, the danger increased for him so she put him in a basket and left him in the river Nile. Prophet Musa kept flowing in the river and got into the gardens of the Egyptian Pharaoh, the Pharaoh's wife adopted him, and he grew under her care. But the Pharaoh was not happy with this as there was a prophecy done in the ancient Egypt that the Pharaoh would be killed by a child born to Israelites (This is the reason Prophet Musa's mother flowed him in the river). So, to check weather this child was the child of prophecy or not he setup a test where Prophet Moses was made to choose between gold and coal (burning). But as we know everything happens by the will of Allah so, Allah made prophet Musa to choose the coal and thus Prophet Musa choose coal and put it to his mouth and this act protected him from the pharaoh. After this the Pharaoh agreed to let her wife adopt him. Prophet Musa grew in the Pharaoh's palace. This Pharaoh was a cruel pharaoh and regarded himself as God, he was merciless and treated people badly, he declined Prophet Musa's teaching of monotheism and to end this cruel pharaoh, Allah nourished a child under the pharaoh's care who would eventually become the reason of his death. Prophet Musa was ordered to free the Israelites and run with them from there to the dead sea. When prophet Musa freed the Israelites and started moving towards the dead sea, The pharaoh and his army chased them and tried to catch them as they thought that Prophet Musa would not be able to cross the sea, but prophet Musa knew that if Allah has ordered him to do something he would surely succeed. So as soon as prophet Musa reached to the red sea with his Israelites, Allah ordered him to hit his staff to the ground and Prophet Musa did the same as he was told. As prophet Musa hit the ground with his stick, the sea split opened and a path was formed for them to cross the sea but the problem was the Pharaoh and his army, the also reached there but as soon as the pharaoh's army tried to cross the sea Allah ordered the sea to go back to its natural form, the sea reformed and the entire army of the pharaoh drowned and a curse was given to the Pharaoh by Allah, that the Pharaoh's body was preserved for the coming people (Tyrants, oppressors, etc.). This story shows us that arrogance is not liked by Allah and shows us that if Allah wants to make something happen, he could make it happen by any means. So be grateful to Allah, don't be arrogant and always ask Allah to take us under his protection.

Prophet Musa was sent with revelation to the Children of Israel to teach them about the one and only god, the sustainer of the whole universe and the master of the Alameen, Allah. But the Children of Israel were wicked, they were surely filled with evilness. Every time Prophet Musa leaves them to go somewhere and when he came back, he would always find them worshiping something new, sometimes it would be fire and sometimes it would be a cow. Children of Israel were meant to spread mischief to the world, and they will continue to do this until the day when they will come to an end, the time accounted by Allah, it would be the last hour and it would be the time after the arrival and killing of the false Messiah, the antichrist, The Dajjal.

No Prophet in Quran is mentioned more than him
More than him is none discussed in it
The one who saved the bani israel[7]
From the unjust tyrant of Egypt

The Prophet who was dark in complexion
and had the strength of ten men
Prophet who used to talk directly with Allah-As-Samee[8]
Only one given the title of Kalim Allah by Allah-Al-Alee[9]

Prophet on whom Torah was revealed
Prophet who comes under the five great[10]
The one who debated with the powerful ruler
With the help of Allah and his unwavering faith

Prophet Isa (Jesus)

Now as for this Prophet no introduction should be needed as he is the one respected by every Abrahamic religion. He is the Prophet who was in the past and will be in the *future*. He is the child who spoke in his cradle. He is the one whom the wicked tried to kill but he will rise again. He is the one who will rise again as an Ummati of Prophet Muhammad (ﷺ). He is the one who was born from the blessed womb of Mariyam AS (Virgin Mary).

He is the worshipper and the Prophet of the one and only god Allah, he is *Isa Ibn e Mariyam*.

Prophet Isa was born by a Blessed woman Mary; she is among the purest people to live on the earth and is the only woman mentioned by name in the Qur'an and has a chapter on her name. After Mariyam was born, her parents died, and Prophet Zakariya AS took Mariyam AS under his care. She used to live in a room in Masjid Al Aqsa in Jerusalem (this is one of the reasons why Al Aqsa is important for all the Abrahamic faiths) and pray there most of the times, she was a very pious woman. One day Angel Gabriel came to her in the form of a man and gave Mariyam glad tidings for the coming of a baby, but Mariyam was confused and asked Allah that she never came into contact with any men so how could she give birth to a baby. Allah told her that this baby was a miracle from Allah and the baby will bear witness in front of all the people who would try to mock you and blame you for adultery. And the same happened when Prophet Isa was born, people blamed Mariyam of adultery but the baby that is Isa AS bear witness and spoke while being in the cradle that her mother is a pious woman and innocent.

Prophet Isa bared witness while in the cradles that his master that is Allah has sent him as a messenger to the bani Israel to guide them and prevent them from wickedness. But there were some leaders among the Bani Israel who feared that this child would take their place, and their wicked business would fail, so they continuously tried to deceive people of Bani Israel and kept on blaming Mariyam of adultery. The feared that Isa AS will now become the new leader and thus they would not be able to deceive people like they did before. They tried their best to build a bad reputation for Isa AS and were somewhat able to succeed but not completely because of the miracles which were provided to Isa AS which forced people to believe in him. He once took some clay, molded it into a bird and then blew into it and it came to live, Subhan Allah. The people of Bani Israel at that time were mastered in medicine but they were not able to completely cure diseases like leper and blindness but Prophet Isa was able to cure leaper and he was also able to cure blindness just by wiping his hands over the blind, he was able to bring the dead back to life and while he did all this, he just said one thing that was it is not me who do all these things, I am just a source the doer is the Almighty Allah. Because of Isa AS guiding people and failing the plans of the false leaders among the Bani Israel, the leaders went to the Roman King who ruled Jerusalem and told him that there is a man who claims to be the messenger of God and is trying to overthrow your crown, knowing this the King ordered his people to capture Isa AS and crucify him (Crucifixion is a way of executing in which a person was put on a cross and his hands and feet are nailed to the cross and then the person is left there to die a slow and painful death). The king's soldier searched for Isa AS (Jesus) and they found him but never forget someone who is blessed by Allah, a person whom Allah created without a father and protected by Allah cannot be harmed by anyone except by the will of Allah, so Allah protected Jesus and Ascended him to the heaven and transformed Jesus's face with a normal person (there are some hadiths related to this man but we will not talk about him due to lack of authentic Hadiths) and when the soldiers reached Jesus's location and searched for him they found the man whose face was transformed into Jesus's, they captured him and took him to the King for crucifixion, the man tried to explain to them that he was not Jesus but the soldiers didn't believed because he had the same face and was hence crucified but it as we know he was not crucified and was Ascended to heaven by

Allah and will be resurrected and his coming will be among the major signs of the final hour.

Now we shall talk about why Jesus is so important for us to know about. Jesus is the prophet who serve as the basis of the three major religions of the world (Islam, Christianity and Judaism). The Jews were those who thought that Jesus was not a good prophet and was rather the false messiah which clearly means that they didn't believe that Jesus was not God. Whereas in Christianity, they believe that Jesus Is part of the Trinity (i.e. he was The Son) and he was the God. While the Muslims believe that Jesus was the rightful messenger of Allah (God) and was sent as a prophet and messenger for the people of Bani Israel and in fact it is obligatory for a person to believe that Jesus was a Prophet sent by Allah, to be a Muslim. It is obligatory for a Muslim to believe in the prophethood of Jesus and to believe that he was ascended to heaven and will be resurrected and will defeat the false Messiah, Dajjal (Major signs of Final Hour). A person who does not believe in all these things is said to lack Imaan (faith). Therefore, we can know from these details that these three religions are same in some way, but the differences came from Jesus and therefore it was important for us to know about him.

What was the response you received
do you remember the favor we did
when we supported you with a pure spirit
and taught you what wisdom really is

So, you spoke to people in your infancy and adulthood
and protected you from the disbeliever's falsehood
by holiest women[11] we brought you to life
by my will you used to make the dead alive

*I have no knowledge indeed
you are the knower of the unseen
I remember your favor of giving me existence
your wisdom taught me how to outdistance*

*My disciples want food from paradise
to get reassured about you
I agreed with them with your advice
waiting for now what you will do*

*Of Course we are ready to send
a table of food straight from heaven
but we'll punish if they still disbelieve in me
the punishment that we haven't given to any being*

*I never said them to worship me and my mother
how could i say of what I don't have any right to utter
you created me just like Prophet Adam by your will
and saved me from disbelievers when they tried me to kill*

*I Never said to worship anyone beside you
I'm just a human messenger of what is true
you know what is hidden within me
but I do not know what is within you*

---

*References...

1) Quran 17:55-Your Lord knows best all those in the heavens and the earth. And We surely favored some prophets over others, and to David we gave the Psalms. (The reason Prophet David is singled out here is because some Jewish authorities at

the time of the prophet Muhammad claimed that no scripture had been revealed after Moses. So, this verse refutes this claim by referring to the Psalms of Prophet David)

2) Islam, Christianity and Judaism

3) Prophet Nuh came before him and that who came after are Prophet Moses, Jesus and Muhammad()

4) Prophet Ishmael

5) Prophet Lut, he was the first to believe in prophet Ibrahim

6) Prophet Muhammad(ﷺ)

7)The Banu Israel are called by this name because Israel was another name for the Prophet Yaqub (Jacob), and from his twelve children came the twelve tribes that constituted Banu Israel. After Yusuf (as) became the minister of Egypt, his whole family migrated there.

8)As-Samee means the all hearer

9)Al-Alee means the most high

10) the five greatest prophets are Prophet Noah, Ibrahim, Moses, Jesus and Muhammad (ﷺ)

11)Maryam (Mary) in Quran 3"42 it says " And 'remember when the angels said, "O Mary! Surely Allah has selected you, purified you, and chosen you over all women of the world. " She is the only woman mentioned by name in the Quran and the only woman that has a chapter named by her in the Quran.

★★★

UNIT III: Quran And the Last Prophet

O Prophet We revealed to you the Book with the Truth for all mankind. So, he who follows the Right Way does so to his own benefit, and he who goes astray, shall hurt only himself by straying. You are not accountable on their behalf. **(QURAN 39:4).** This book "**QURAN**" isn't only for the one who is Muslim or the one who believes in ALLAH. This book is for All THE MANKIND. Anyone interested can go through it and there aren't any restrictions to stop anyone from reading it.

Prophet Muhammad (ﷺ) was the last messenger to come, no more will ever come on earth except the second coming of prophet Isa (Jesus). The last prophet taught the Islam in the original form like the previous prophets, but their nations changed their scriptures and message according to their convenience at large.

IV

QURAN

Indeed Allah, through this Book, raises some peoples and lowers others."

(Sahih Muslim 966)

It can be noticed that in recent times people are getting more involved in self-help books than ever before. Yes, it is a good thing to read self-help books as they build great character and make you disciplined. But the thing is that people are not reading the best of the self-help books, which are the holy books of different religions. Each holy book contains a great amount of knowledge in them but today we are going to talk about the holy book of Islam, The Al-Furqan, The Quran. Many ideas in this book which you are reading right now are derived from the Holy Quran.

The Quran was revealed to the Last Prophet, Prophet Muhammad (ﷺ). It is a book which was given to the entire mankind as a source of guidance, it was meant to help mankind. It is the ultimate source of knowledge. It gives you the step-by-step guide to come closer to Allah and make your way into Jannah. The Quran contains many teachings, which are not only necessary for the Akhirah but also for the current Duniya. It tells about the way of discipline, the way of peace, the way of truthfulness, the way from which you should maintain a distance and it tells you about the most important thing " Halal and Haram". If a person follows the Quran he can never be distressed, he can never be sad, he will see the world from a different point of view, he will not harm anyone, he will not oppress anyone, ultimately, he will live a life of happiness. The Quran tells us about how we can create good relations with our family, Neighbours, friends and life partners. It tells us how we should treat people. It tells us that no person shall oppress any other person. Every person has his/her own rights, and no other person can violate those rights.

The Quran provides you with the knowledge of different problems. It tells you about the Right of Property, Halal and Haram, Human rights, Marriage and many more. The Quran has given many scientific proofs which were stated in the Quran more than 1400 years ago and were discovered by scientists recently. Some of those are:

(i) Two seas have a separation between them, their qualities such as temperature and density are different from each other. **(Qur'an 55:19-20)**
(ii) Iron is not native to earth. It came from the outside. **(Qur'an 57:25)**
(iii) The Universe keeps expanding itself. **(Qur'an 51:47)**
This proves the authenticity, and the great wisdom stored in the Quran. Not only these, but the Quran has also mentioned many more scientific miracles like these. Apart from the Duniya, the Quran tells us about various things which are important for us for the Akhirah. The Quran tells us about everything in eternity. It constantly reminds us that there is a life after this mortal life which will remain, The Life of Akhirah. It tells us about the torment/hardships of the grave, it tells us about the situation of The Day of Judgement, it tells us about the horrifying Jahannam, and it tells us about the peaceful and beautiful life of the Jannah as well. But we can enter Jannah only if we stand strong as a believer, do what is mentioned in the Quran and prepare for the

Akhirah, The Eternity. Indeed, The Quran is presented to us in a way by which we can prepare for the Akhirah. So, brothers and sisters, not only read the Quran but also understand it and do as it is stated in The Quran. This life will end but the life after this life won't. Quran was revealed to guide you so let it.

The book revealed by the lord of heaven and earth
Not to cause you distress or to hurt
But one in awe of God as a reminder
And as a warner for the denier

Revealed in Ramadan on a blessed night[1]
To set standard between wrong and right
Superior to previous scriptures[2] with no Doubt
And to teach you humanity throughout

If Allah wouldn't have created it
it would be inconsistent from beginning to end
If All of us come together and unite
We can't produce anything like or transcend

A revelation that fills the believer with tears
and trembles the heart of the one who fears
A revelation where mercy is mentioned twice,
times of the; word punishment appears

It is certainly We Who have revealed the Reminder, and it is certainly We Who will preserve it.

(Quran 15:9)

V

THE LAST PROPHET

And we sent you (O Muhammad) not but as a mercy for the alamin (mankind. Jinn and all that exists)

(Quran 21:107)

Prophets played an important role in spreading religion and guiding people. Allah has sent many messengers and prophets to guide the people of different eras, and we also know that each prophet/messenger was the purest among their people. But what if we talk about a prophet in which's Ummah, another prophet wanted to be a part of. Sounds strange but it isn't. Because here we are talking about the purest man, the greatest man to ever live on planet earth, we are talking about a man who converted a wicked city where female child were considered as a burden, where women were oppressed, where zina(adultery) was common, where people were alcoholic to a city which is now considered as the purest city in the whole world, it became a city where daughters have now become the reason for a man to enter Jannah, it became a city where women are now their husband's best friend, it became a city where whoever commits zina is punished, it became a city where even selling alcohol is a crime. We are talking about our Prophet Muhammad (ﷺ). Prophet Muhammad (ﷺ) was the last prophet sent by Allah and there will be no prophet after him [except the second coming of Prophet Isa (Jesus) as the part of Prophet's Ummah], but people misinterpret this they think that Islam started from Muhammad (1400 years ago) but in actually Islam (worshipping the only God Allah) started from Adam(The first human Being on Earth) and all the prophets and Messengers from Adam AS to Prophet Muhammad (ﷺ) preached the monotheism religion(Worshipping the only God Allah).

If we began with the topic of our Prophet Muhammad (ﷺ), the discussion on him will take volumes to complete yet it won't be completed. So here only four aspects of his life which are his qualities, honors bestowed on him, challenges he faced and some lessons by him are briefly explained to know about the wonderful human being.

Qualities

You may wonder what makes us say that Prophet Muhammad (ﷺ) was the purest man or the most wonderful human being? It is his qualities which made him so pure and wonderful. He was so generous, sincere and kind that he was known as The Truthful One in the wicked city of Mecca and was among the Most respectful people of Mecca even before the Prophethood was bestowed on him. Although After his Prophethood was announced and he started to preach Islam, people mocked him, tortured him and even tried to kill him but he never got angry with them and always asked Allah to turn their hearts away from evil and guide them. He was a very loving person and was good towards children, women and his companions/people. He was so caring towards his companions that they used to say that they never felt more loved than when sitting with the prophet. Although he was the leader of the Muslims but he was unlike the other leaders who make their men work and sit behind and watch them work, he used to work with his companions, there was a battle called the Battle of Trench in which people dug a trench to fight with the enemies and prophet Muhammad (ﷺ) also took part in digging the trench. He was not unjust; he treated everyone equally. He was completely against the unfair treatment towards the servants, he taught the people that whatever you eat should be given to your servants, whatever you wear should be given to your servants. And the most important quality of Prophet Muhammad (ﷺ) was patience, he faced many challenges in his life while spreading Islam, but he tackled them all with one single thing which is patience and belief in the plan of Allah. He lost many of his loved ones in the battles against the Kuffar, but he didn't disbelieve in the plan of Allah and was patient all along and as a result we can see that the Islam which he was spreading has now become the fastest growing religion in the world and the second biggest religion.

Muhammad is no more than a messenger
there were other messengers before him too
he isn't an angel, but a man like us
but a man with a revelation which is true

A prophet not sent as a keeper over us
but a deliverer of news which is good
A noble man who spread peace
a man who spread brotherhood

A prophet sent to the world as mercy
and as a great favour which none can overcome
An astonishing man who leads to the straight path
by teaching the book of ultimate wisdom

A prophet to be followed and to behold
a man about whom even Jesus foretold
The description about whom they find in previous books[3]
a different man with a different outlook

Honors bestowed

Prophet Muhammad (ﷺ) was an honored man and the biggest honor of his is being the Beloved of The Almighty Allah. Prophet Muhammad (ﷺ) is honored in many ways; he is the Prophet before whom many prophets and Messengers came but after him there is none. He is marked as the seal of the prophets, he is the last prophet whom Allah Almighty sent to guide the people, after him there is no one to guide the people except his (Prophet Muhammad (ﷺ)) teachings and the Divine Scripture, Qur'an. The Qur'an is another honor bestowed on Prophet Muhammad (ﷺ) as it is the Divine Scripture from The Almighty to guide the entire Aalamin (Humans and Jinns). Prophet Muhammad (ﷺ) was also honoured with many titles like An-Niamatullah (The divine favour of Allah), As-Shaheed (The witness), Al-Mubashir (The bearer of good tidings) and Khalilullah (The friend Of Allah). He was also provided with divine wisdom from his lord (The Almighty Allah).

A very important and significant miracle of the Prophet Muhammad (ﷺ) is The Night Journey or the Isra Wal Meraj. In this journey, the prophet first went to Jerusalem and from there he went to the heavens where he met different prophets at different levels and after that he went to The Sidra Tul Muntaha and then he was instructed by Allah about the five daily prayers. And all this happened within the duration of a single night.

By the Stars when they fade away
your fellow man[4] is neither misguided nor astray
nor does he speak of his own whims
it is only a revelation sent down to him[5]

A prophet whom both God and Angels bless
a man honored in this life and the next

the one who met the prophets during the journey of night[6]
a man who was honored with the greatest of height

Whoever obeys the messenger has truly obeyed God
And the one who does it will in company of those who God blessed[7]
the one who obeys what's ordered from the lord
Are the ones who will be heavenly addressed

A prophet preceded by Jesus
and a prophet succeeded by none
a man honored as beloved, honest and the witness
a man honored as kind, noble and the praised one[8]

Challenges

There is a famous saying that wherever there is good there is evil too. Same goes here, although prophet Muhammad (ﷺ) was among the most respected people of Mecca but after his Prophethood was established, people forced him to leave the city where he was born. People of Mecca tortured him in every possible way, they mocked him, threw intestines of animals on him and what not. People of Mecca tried to assassinate him because of his preaching of monotheism and opposing of paganism and idolatry performed by the Pagan Arabs, due to this the leaders of Mecca, including his own Uncle, Abu Lahab become his blood thirsty enemies, they fought with him, made him leave his beloved city and restricted his entry in Mecca. Even after the prophet (ﷺ) migrated to Medina, the Arab leaders didn't stop and launched battles with him, like the Battle of Badr, Battle of Uhud and Battle of Trench. But they all resulted with the defeats of the Pagan Arab leaders. The battle of Uhud was one of the most important battles in which the prophet faced a major loss of his blood related beloved Uncle Hazrat Hamza.

During his whole life he faced many challenges, whether it be battles or just people's rebellious behavior towards him for preaching Islam. One such incident is from the early times of Prophethood, where prophet Muhammad (ﷺ) moved to Taif to spread Islam(monotheism) but the people of Taif not only rejected him, but they also pelted him with stones causing him to bleed. But the prophet didn't let this incident stop him and he forgave them for what they had done and continued his preaching of the one true monotheist religion.

The tenth year of the prophethood was another year which was very difficult for the prophet (ﷺ), during this year the prophet lost his wife Hazrat Khadija RA and also faced the death of his beloved Uncle Hazrat Abu Talib, who took care of prophet Muhammad (ﷺ) since his childhood and was among the first few people who believed in him and was always there to protect him from the pagans and disbelievers. This year of Prophethood is known as the Year of Sorrow. There are several more challenges which he faced in order to establish the Islam that we see now but what are we doing? We are just taking Islam for granted because we didn't have to face those challenges, we are leaving our prayers and indulging in wrong doings (Shirk, Zina, Riba, oppressing others, etc.). Just imagine if you were at the time of the prophet and faced the same challenges that he faced, would you still be doing the things you are today involved in? Would you still be leaving your prayers just because you don't feel like praying? Would you still be cursing people just because they didn't agree with your opinion? Would you still be lying on your bed and scroll for several hours just because you are getting that cheap dopamine?

Pagans demanded prophet to make the angles to come
they prayed to God to let stones rain down[9]
they say why prophet for a living has to move around[10]
they call you by names[11] *look how astray they have*
become

They accused him as magician, fabricator, liar,
fortune teller, poet and a mad man
to kill him they used to plan and conspire
but God is the best of those who plan

Those who defy God's message and mock prophet that
he spread lies
surely, they will have a beautiful ends[12]
you(prophet) deal with patience with the one who
denies
you deal with patience with the one who offends

we (Allah) certainly know that your (prophet)
heart is distressed by what they say
so, glorify the praises of your lord
and be one of those who always pray[13]

Lessons

Prophet Muhammad was a very influential Human Being. He is like a role model for the Ummah, he taught us various things and also, we can learn a lot from the way he ((ﷺ)) used to live. The first and one of the things we lack the most today that we can learn from the Prophet is HONESTY. Prophet Muhammad (ﷺ) was a very honest man, so much so that he was known as The Truthful One in Mecca even before his Prophethood. In today's world, lying is common, people tell lies without even hesitating, they lie while selling things, the tell lies while talking about an incident, they lie to make someone feel inferior, they even lie to destroy someone's life/career, and they even lie to destroy families. Lies are the scariest things if we look at them with a normal point of view but we don't. We think that lying is common and we should lie too, but we don't think that what if someone lies to us, we don't like it if someone lies to us, but we lie ourselves. So, to improve ourselves, we should be honest, we should always try to or be able to speak the truth even if it is against us because a true and honest man never faces backlashes, he would never regret what he has said. The essence of truth and honesty is beautiful and whoever has this essence is indeed a true definition of a beautiful person.

Another thing that we can learn from Prophet Muhammad (ﷺ) is patience and forgiveness. As we have come across some of the challenges faced by the prophet Muhammad (ﷺ), we can notice something, that no matter the hardships, he always kept living the life the same way, he kept preaching Islam no matter how many times people rejected him, no matter what people called him, he was patient and his patience didn't stumbled no matter how hard time gets. Patience is needed in everything, whether you want to earn money, build a great physique or practice your religion. Patience is the key to success even Allah states in the Qur'an that Allah is with those who are patient (Qur'an 2-153). People today, get angry on small things, they tend to fight even on small things, they hardly have any feeling of forgiveness in their hearts, they think that if they let a person go they will appear weak whereas even though the people of Taif wounded the Prophet, he (ﷺ) forgave him, He was the leader of the Muslims, he was beloved of the Almighty Allah, he could destroy the people of Taif but what did he do? He forgave them for their doing. We need to understand that forgiving someone or apologizing to someone does not make us inferior.

Prophet Muhammad (ﷺ) also told us to be good with our families and neighbors. If we are eating something and our neighbor is going to sleep with an empty stomach it is our responsibility to not let him sleep empty stomach. If Allah has bestowed blessings (food, cloth, shelter, etc.) on you, then it is your responsibility to help your neighbors who need anything. Prophet Muhammad (ﷺ) told us to be good with kids and our wives. Prophet Muhammad (ﷺ) taught us to treat our wives well, he told us to love our wives and not cause any trouble to them, he taught us to take care of our wives, help them in whatever thing we are able to and provide a safe environment for them.

Now that we have come across the brief about the life of Prophet Muhammad (ﷺ), we should ask ourselves, what can we learn from him? Actually, there is a lot to learn from him (ﷺ), but the question should be, can we implement the things we learned from Prophet Muhammad (ﷺ)? Because without implementation of a thing that we learn is the same as knowing everything about driving a car, but you can't actually drive it. So, the things which we have learned from this chapter, you should start implementing it, may it be just any one of his teachings, but you should be consistent, you should keep implementing his teachings even in a small amount. Remember, a house is built by placing several small bricks regularly and not just by placing a big one.

There are various lessons to learn
from the prophet which concern
about the life and it's way of living
about the art of apology and forgiving

To donate and to give charity
to speak truth and too with clarity
to be fair in business and kind with neighborhood
to do not criticize and mind the brotherhood

He said to honor and respect your women
and fear Allah in regarding her too
and told a reward of a house in heaven
for the one being right but still gives up to argue

Say (O Muhammad to mankind) if you (really)love Allah
then follow me (i e. accept Islamic monotheism follow the
Quran and the Sunnah) Allah will love you ...

(Quran 3:31)

VI

LAST SERMON OF PROPHET MOHAMMED S.A.W

Prophet Muhammad (ﷺ) said convey (Knowledge) from me even it is just a single verse.

(Bukhari 3461)

After praising and thanking Allah the **Prophet Mohammed (ﷺ)** began with the words:

"O People! Lend me an attentive ear, for I know not whether after this year I shall ever be amongst you again. Therefore, listen carefully to what I am saying and take these words to those who could not be present here today."

"O People! Just as you regard this month, this day, this city as sacred, so regard the life and property of every Muslim a sacred trust. Return the goods entrusted to you to their rightful owners. *Hurt no one so that no one may hurt you*. Remember that you will indeed meet your Lord, and that he will indeed reckon your deeds."

"Allah has forbidden you to take usury, therefore all interest obligation shall henceforth be waived. Your capital is yours to keep. You will neither inflict nor suffer any inequality. Allah has judged that there shall be no interest and that all interest due to Abbas Ibn 'Abd al-Muttalib be waived."

"Every right arising out of homicide in pre-Islamic days is henceforth waived and the first such right that I waive is that arising from the murder of Rabiah ibn al-Harithiah."

"**O men**! the unbelievers indulge in tampering with the calendar in order to make permissible that which Allah forbade, and to prohibit what Allah has made permissible. With Allah the months are twelve in number. Four of them are holy, there are successive, and one occurs singly between the months of Jumada and Shaban."

"*Beware of Satan, for the safety of your religion. He has lost all hope that he will be able to lead you astray in big things so beware of following him in small things.*"

"**O People** it is true that you have certain rights with regard to your women, but they also have rights over you. Remember that you have taken them as your wives only under Allah's trust and with His permission. If they abide by your right, then to them belongs the right to be fed and clothed in kindness. *Do treat your women well and be kind to them for they are your partners and committed helpers.* And it is your right that they do not make friends with any one of whom you do not approve, as well never to be unchaste."

"O People! listen to me in earnest, worship Allah, say your five daily prayers, fast during the month of Ramadan, and give your wealth in Zakat. Perform Haj if you can afford it."

"All mankind is from Adam and Eve, an Arab has no superiority over a non-Arab nor a non-Arab has any superiority over an Arab; also, a White has no superiority over a Black nor a Black has any superiority over a White except by piety and good action. Learn that every Muslim is a brother to every Muslim and that the Muslims constitute one brotherhood. Nothing shall be legitimate to a Muslim which belongs to a fellow Muslim unless it was given freely and willingly."

"Do not therefore do injustice to yourselves. Remember one day you will meet Allah and answer your deeds. So beware, do not astray from the path of righteousness after I am gone."

"O People! No Prophet or apostle will come after me and no new faith will be born. Reason well, therefore *O People! and understand words that I convey to you. I leave behind me two things, the Quran and the Sunnah and if you follow these you will never go astray."*

"All those who listen to me shall pass on my words to others and those to others again; and may the last ones understand my words better than those who listen to me directly."

"O Allah, be my witness, that I have conveyed your message to Your people."

As part of this sermon, the prophet recited to them a revelation from Allah, which he had just received, and which completed the Quran, for it was the last passage to be revealed:

This day the disbeliever's despair of prevailing against your religion, so fear them not, but fear Me (Allah)! This day have I perfected for you, your religion and fulfilled My favor unto you, and it hath been My good pleasure to choose Islam for you as your religion. (Surah 5, Ayah 3)

The sermon was repeated sentence by sentence by Safwan's brother Rabiah (RA), who had a powerful voice, at the request of the Prophet and he faithfully proclaimed to over ten thousand gathered on the occasion. Towards the end of his sermon, the Prophet asked, "O people, have I faithfully delivered unto you, my message?" A powerful murmur of assents "O Allah! yes! "Arose from thousands of pilgrims and the vibrant words "Allahumma Na'm," rolled like thunder throughout the valley. The Prophet raised his forefinger and said: "O Allah bear witness that I have conveyed your message to your people."

O people,
Give me an attentive ear

listen carefully to what I say
and take these words to those who aren't here today
for I might not be amongst you again
So let me share what Allah has ordain

Satan has no hope to lead you in big things
So, in small, he will try to mislead
indeed, you will meet you lord at the end
indeed, he will reckon your all your deed

Hurt no one, so no one may hurt you
you have right on your women and theirs over you
Fast during Ramadan and Worship the Almighty
give wealth in zakat, and offer prayers too

No one is superior except by piety
and deeds which are good
All the Muslims are brothers
and constitute one brotherhood

O Allah, Bear witness that I have conveyed your message
to your people

***Reference.**

1)27th night of Ramadan

2)Torah, Gospel and Zabur

3)Some Muslims scholars cite Deuteronomy18:15-18 and 33:2, Isaiah 42, and John 14:16 as examples of the description of prophet Muhammad in the Bible.

4) Prophet Muhammad

5) Quran 53:1-4

6)Al-Isra, the night Journey when he went to Jerusalem and then to heavens where Allah ordered the five daily prayers

7) The one blessed by the Allah are the people of truth martyrs and the righteous

8) The prophet was given many titles by Allah, prophet companions and the people of Arab

9)Quran 8:32,33 (in these two verse the pagans asked to rain down stones, but Allah would never do such while the prophet was amongst them)

10) Prophet used to eat food and goes in marketplaces for living like all the other humans do because prophet himself too was human, but the pagans used to mock him on this

11) pagans used to call prophet as magician, liar etc.

12) severe punishment and hell, the word beautiful is used in a sarcastic way

13)Quran 15:97

14)The Last Sermon of Prophet Muhammad ()

This sermon was delivered on the Ninth day of Dhul-Hijja, 10 A.H. (623 AD) in the Uranah valley of Mount Arafat in Mecca. It was the occasion for the annual rites of Hajj. It is also known as the Farewell Pilgrimage.

Credit:-

https://www.iium.edu.my/deed/articles/thelastsermon.html

✸✸✸

UNIT IV: Basic Pillars

*But without basic pillars a building can't stand,
and without pillars a structure can't be formed.
Some help it to form, some help by giving assistance.
which helps to do good, and to stop bad by giving resistance*

The structure will remain hollow even if the pillars are strong as there are no walls that are good deeds to protect the person living inside that is Faith from the strong deviants living outside which are Bad Desires, Media, and Bad Deeds. And if the walls are created there are Windows and doors created too.

The windows refer to the Satan that whispers in your ears to see the worldly life outside and the doors are like the guardian of faith which leads you to different destinations one to Hell and another to Heaven.

Even if you build strong pillars for your faith, you must create walls by doing good deeds and try to be away from the bad ones to protect your faith, but one part of the Structure is still left and what is it? It is the roof. If it Isn't there then the other part of that structure has no worth. And what that Roof is? Roof is the one in whom you believe in.

And what's the name of the structure formed?

" Religion "

In Islam there are Five basic pillars but here only two are discussed, which are Salah and Pilgrimage.

VII

SALAH

"Between a man and polytheism and disbelief there stands his neglect of the prayer."

(Sahih Muslim 82a)

Salah has a major importance in a believer's life, and one of one of the five pillars of Islam. It is the most important thing for being a Muslim after the Shahadah (believe in the oneness of ALLAH. Salah is a way through which we, the servants of Allah, can connect to our god, ask him for help, forgiveness, guidance and thank him for all his bounties he has provided for us and what he will provide in future. It is mandatory to offer Salah (five daily prayers) for believers. Salah is the first thing that differentiates a believer from a non-believer. Also, offering it on their earliest stated times is the dearest to Allah **(Sahih Al Bukhari 527).** If a person neglects it with intention, not only he breaks the direct connection with Almighty but also destroys his faith completely. Therefore, Salah shouldn't be neglected as it destroys our faith and moves us away from the Al-Razzaq (The provider i.e. Allah). Salah is the key to Jannah. Allah says in the Qur'an that the people of the hellfire would be asked, "What had landed you here." They will answer that we were of those who didn't pray **(Qur'an 74:38-43).** It will be the first thing about which you would be enquired on the day of judgment and the rest of your rest deeds after it **(Sunan al-Tirmidhī 413).** So, it is better for you to punctually offer Salah and do not leave it intentionally. Remember, the easiest way to clear a test is to prepare for it. The test of Akhirah is far more difficult than the worldly tests so, offer it sincerely so that you could clear the test of the Akhirah with ease.

Let us now look at its importance and benefits apart from the Islamic point of view. Salah helps us to disconnect with the worldly desires and makes us connected to what is eternal. It can be considered as a form of meditation, it disconnects us from all distractions, provides peace to our souls, gives us a reason to live and helps in building character as well as discipline. It also makes a person punctual, focused toward his/her tasks and builds a great routine. It helps you to wake up early in the morning and to sleep early and perform all tasks on time. Many people think like that Salah will give them less time to do other work, but it is indeed a wrong fact because if you offer Salah, you will gradually start to feel that you are able to do other work on time and manage everything on time. Once you get a habit of Salah, it will be the best thing for you.

Al-Isra Wal Meraj

The reason and how 5 daily prayers were made obligated on the believers can be derived from the following incident. During the journey of Meraj [The journey of prophet (ﷺ) where he went to Masjid Al Aqsa (Palestine), where he met other prophets and in the last met Allah], Prophet (ﷺ) met other prophets and talked with them after which Prophet (ﷺ) went to meet Allah. There, 50 daily prayers were enjoined on the believers after this Prophet (ﷺ)went back to Musa AS. Musa AS said to him that these prayers are too much for your Ummah and you Ummah cannot keep with this obligation, Musa AS told him to return to Allah and ask him to reduce the number of prayers. Prophet (ﷺ) went back, and Allah reduced the prayers to 40. Now, prophet (ﷺ)one more time went to Musa AS, this time Musa AS told the exact same thing after that Prophet (ﷺ) went back, and asked Allah to reduce the prayers and Allah reduced it to 30. This continued, the prayers got reduced to 20 to 10 and finally to 5. But this time also Musa AS asked Prophet (ﷺ) to ask Allah to reduce the prayers even more, but this time Prophet(ﷺ)replied that I have surrendered to Allah's final order. Therefore, the Five daily prayers were made obligatory on the Ummah. **(Sahih Bukhari 3207, Book 59, Hadith 18).**

Five Hadiths About the five mandatory daily prayers:

Fajr- "The two Rak'ah before the dawn (Fajr) prayer are better than this world and all it contains. **"Riyad as-Salihin 1102**

Zuhr-"In very hot weather delay the Zuhr prayer till it becomes (a bit) cooler because the severity of heat is from the raging of Hellfire. Volume 1, Book 10, Number 512.

Asr- "Whoever misses the `Asr prayer (intentionally) then it is as if he lost his family and property. **"Sahih al-Bukhari 552**

Maghrib-The Messenger of Allah said: 'My Ummah will continue to adhere to the Fitrah so long as they do not delay the Maghrib until the stars have come out."... **Sunan ibn majah 689.**

Isha-"Whoever attends Isha (prayer) in congregation, then he has (the reward as if he had) stood half of the night. And whoever prays Isha and Fajr in congregation, then he has (the reward as if he had) spend the entire night standing (in prayer)." **Jami` at-Tirmidhi 221**.

Tahajjud

Apart from these obligatory prayers there are more prayers, which we can offer for extra rewards or to ask Allah for something we wish. Tahajjud is the prime example of this type of prayer. Prophet Muhammad (ﷺ) said, "During the last third remaining time of the night, Allah comes down to the nearest heavens and says "Is there anyone to ask me for something? So, I provide him with that. Is there anyone to ask forgiveness from me? So that I forgive him." **(Sahih Bukhari 1145, Book 19, Hadith 26).** This shows the power of the tahajjud prayer and the love of Allah Al Wadud, the most loving, and tells us that we should ask Allah for anything we want in the Tahajjud. Prayers hold extraordinary powers in them, they connect you with your God and turn you into a better personality.

Seek help through patience and prayer
Pray at the time of joy or despair
Pray for those who are in digress
And pray often, you may get success

Indeed, righteous are those who pray
And doomed are those who disobey

Establish prayer at both ends of day
And in early part of the night[1]
Pray at time of calmness
And pray when you get fright

Indeed, righteous are those who pray
And doomed are those who disobey.

Whenever someone is touched by hardship, they cry out to Us, whether lying on their side, sitting, or standing. But when We relieve their hardship, they return to their old ways as if they had never cried to Us to remove any hardship! This is how the misdeeds of the transgressors have been made appealing to them. (Quran 10 :12)

VIII

PILGRIMAGE

Indeed, the first House [of worship] established for mankind was that at Makkah - blessed and a guidance for the worlds.

(Quran 3:96)

Pilgrimage also known as a spiritual journey done by a person to a religious place of great importance. Pilgrimage is almost common in every religion, people from different religions go to their different places of worship, whether it be a Mosque, a Temple, or a Church.

In Islam pilgrimage to the two holy mosques, The Haram (Kaaba) in Mecca and Masjid Nabawi in Medina is very common where there is one pilgrimage which is obligatory/mandatory for every believer which is Hajj (In Mecca), and the second pilgrimage is a non-mandatory one which is Umrah. In both, the main city is the land of Mecca. Pilgrimage (Hajj) is one of the five pillars of Islam, that is why it is also mandatory. But apart from Salah which everyone must perform irrespective of the situation, Hajj is only mandatory on those who can afford it either financially, physically or mentally. The main difference between the two pilgrimages is the timing, where Umrah can be performed as many times as possible, but Hajj can only be performed once every year on a specified date (9 of Zill Hijja). Umrah is an expiation from the sins done between it and the previous one (Volume 3, Book 27, Number 1). But in this topic, we are specifically going to know about hajj. Why is it important and its significance?

Now, Hajj has a very great significance, Prophet (ﷺ) said that whoever performs Hajj for the sake of Allah and does not have any intimate relationship with his wife, does not do any evil deed and stays away from any type of sin during Hajj, then Allah will forgive all his prior sins and the person would become like he is a newborn baby i.e. free of any sin. **(Sahih Bukhari 1521 and Muslim 1350).**

Before moving further let us know what Hajj Mabrur is. This is a Hajj which is accepted by Allah, a Hajj by which Allah is pleased. This can be done only by the conditions we have talked about earlier (do not have any intimate relationship with your wife, do not do any evil deed and stay away from any type of sin during Hajj). Now that we know what Hajj Mabrur is, we can understand the following Hadith. Prophet (ﷺ)said that the reward for a Hajj Mabrur is nothing except The Paradise (Volume 3, Book 27, Number 1), which is indeed the best place for the whole mankind. This shows us the significance of Hajj. Allah says in the **Quran, "(3:96)** Behold, the first House (of Prayer) established for mankind is the one at Becca (now Mecca): it is full of blessing and a center of guidance for the whole world. **(3:97)** In it there are clear signs and the station of Abraham; whoever enters it becomes secure. Pilgrimage to the House is a duty owed to Allah by all who can make their way to it.

In it are clear signs [such as] the standing place of Abraham. And whoever enters it shall be safe. And [due] to Allah from the people is a pilgrimage to the House - for whoever is able to find there a way. But whoever disbelieves - then indeed, Allah is free from the need of the worlds.

(Quran 3:97)

Pilgrimage is one of the Islamic Pillar
Obligatory for the one who is able to
Not for the one who can't
Major one is, minor one isn't to do[2]

Don't use foul language and arguments at time of it
(Pilgrimage)
And stay away from intimate relation
Whatever good you do, Allah fully knows of it
Be mindful of Allah oh people of reason!

The one who performs hajj
Will return with no sins as if born anew[3]
The performer of it are many
But Allah might accept of only few

---

*Reference ...

1)This line talks about the five daily prayers. The prayers at the two ends of the day are the dawn prayer (fajr) at the end and the afternoon prayers (Zuhr and Asr) at the other. Prayers in the early part of the night include the sunset (maghrib) and the late evening
(Isha) prayers. It is written in (Quran 11:114)

2)Major one is known as Hajj and minor one is known as Umrah and only hajj is obligatory, not umrah.

3)Narrated Abu Huraira by that The Prophet (p.b.u.h) said Whoever performs Hajj for Allah and does not do evil or sins then he will return (after Hajj free from all sins) as if he were born anew (Sahih-Al-Bukhari: Volume 2, Book 26, Number 596)

UNIT V: Major Issue

October 7 was never the beginning at all. It all started when Jews were roaming all around the world after the mass destruction made by Adolf Hitler and the only nation that welcomed them happily was the nation Palestine. The war started after it. The war didn't begin after the October 7 attack made by Hamas.

Every Oppression has resilience/resistance

that doesn't make the weaker side terrorist

Killing women and children even if the enemy Is hiding inside their building can't be supported and tolerated. Calling the genocide a response of what happened on October 7 is a shame. People getting buried inside the building and getting their body parts blown off begging to die is absolutely unjust. It doesn't matter on which political side you fall on when you see a genocide and see women and children die you must be disgusted.

IX

PALESTINE

"Consider not that Allah is unaware of that which the wrongdoers do, but He gives them respite up to a Day when the eyes will stare in horror."

(Qur'an 14:42)

For a better understanding of this topic, let's move back to the early 1900's, when every Jew was running for his/her life. They didn't have any shelter of their own, asking other countries to give them shelter. But every country declined to keep Jews with them, no one agreed to keep them in their country. That time Britain had control over Palestine, they sent the Jews to live in Palestine and the people of Palestine also agreed to keep them in their country. Palestinians kept them in their country like they were also the citizens of that country. And from that day, Palestine is paying for its kindness till now.

Palestine is of great importance in Islam, as it is the place where Al-Aqsa is located. It is the place where Qibla-e-Awwal is located, the first direction where Muslims faced while offering Salah. It is the place where our Prophet Muhammad (ﷺ) went from Mecca on the blessed night of Meraj **(Quran, 17:1).** It is the place where the people of Israel are leading corruption. As it is mentioned in Quran that the people of Israel will lead corruption in the world **(Qur'an 14:4-6)** and this can be seen through Palestine in the recent times. Israel is planning to destroy the Al Aqsa in order to construct their third temple.

Now we should talk about the real reason of this war which has been triggered long since the day Jews entered Palestine. We all know somewhere that Israel is wrong but most of us are afraid to talk about it in public. Israel has been continuously taking over the land of Palestine slowly from the very first day. Jerusalem is a place of importance for all the Abrahamic faiths. For Christians it is important because Jerusalem is the place where Jesus was crucified and was ascended to the heavens, and for Jews it is the presence of the Holy Wall of theirs. It is the Jew's conspiracy or so-called belief that the land of Jerusalem (Palestine) is their holy land, it is the place of their Third temple and that Al Aqsa was built after destroying their temple and Al-Aqsa should be demolished for the reincarnation of their temple. They want to demolish Al-Aqsa to build the Solomon temple of theirs. For achieving their purpose, they have completely gone off the humanitarian grounds and are killing children, women and men without any reason. Another big reason is the militant group of Gaza called Hamas. Israel in the name of attacking Hamas has killed thousands of innocent children and people in such a small period. And the sad thing with this is that they are not even guilty of what they are doing and people from some parts of the world are supporting Israel in this injustice not understanding what they feel will when someone will do this type of injustice on their country, their children, women and men. People should be shameful of what they are supporting. They are just supporting a Genocide, literally a Genocide. We should not think that they are just killing Muslims, but we should think about the injustice which is not humane at all for any living being, this type of ill treatment is not even tolerable for animals, and they are doing it with children and women. In Islam it is a concept that people who support the wrongdoers are themselves the wrongdoers. We should think about this whole topic wisely not as a person of a different religious group but as a human. I think that nonviolence is the main teaching of every religion. Then why are people supporting this Genocide?

Israel not only is targeting Al-Aqsa, but they are also heartlessly killing innocent children and women, who are not able to protect themselves. They are killing children without any reason. The whole war doesn't have any reason. They have done the most inhumane things, they have committed War Crimes by bombing hospitals, the basic need for the people during a war. They are bombing hospitals, mosques and universities yet many countries are standing with Israel. What will happen if someone destroys your place of worship, schools or place of medications, you will not be able to tolerate it. But at last, maybe Israel has the support of many superpowers, but we should not forget that Palestine has the greatest superpower standing with them, who is ALLAH.

A nation that welcomed Jews
When no other nation did
Is paying the price for years
For the kindness they did

Won't you take any action if someone tries to harm
you or your closed one, yes you will
Aren't the people of Palestine
Getting oppressed and killed, then why you stand still

O Arab nations or those who supported Ukraine
Have you now gone to sleep
What's wrong with your ears now
That you don't hear Palestinian children's weep

Would we like to be separated
From our family or loved one, yes, we won't
If prophet (*) mentioned us as one ummah*
Then why we don't

Are they supposed to be oppressed
Or to be killed
Aren't they supposed to enjoy
And why not their wishes be fulfilled?

Allah's Apostle said, "Help your brother, whether he is an oppressor or he is an oppressed one. People asked, "O Allah's Apostle! It is all right to help him if he is oppressed, but how should we help him if he is an oppressor?" The Prophet said, "By preventing him from oppressing others."

(Sahih al-Bukhari 2444)

★★★

UNIT VI: End Of Time

Hell, and Paradise is believed by all the religions, but judgment day isn't. Everyone that was born will die, some will be buried, some will be burned and some neither of both. Death is inevitable which comes by its time, so does the Day of Judgment. In Islam day of judgment is the day when justice will be served, the righteous will shine, and the wicked will beg. The oppressed will smile, and the Tyrant will cry and so on.

Hell, and paradise according to their deed with the best justice will be given. They will live the life (akhira) with no death some in happiness some in torment.

X

DEATH

The Prophet drew a few lines and said, "This is (man's) hope, and this is the instant of his death, and while he is in this state (of hope), the nearer line (death) comes to Him."

(Sahih al-Bukhari 6418)

Death is something which is common to all. There is nothing in this world which will not taste death, whether it is a Human, an Animal, A plant or anything. Everything will die. No one can escape death, death is universal and will get you on your prescribed time no matter where you go, no matter where you hide.

Many people think that death is the end, but they tend to forget that it is just the beginning. It is the very first step of eternal life. After death the real things start, the question answer of grave, the torment of grave, etc. Also, Death can be of two types, it can either be a peaceful one or it can be terrifying one. It all depends on the deeds of the person. If the person did bad deeds throughout his lifetime then the Angel Of Death (Israel AS) will capture that person's soul in a very painful way, whereas on the other hand if the person did good deeds then Israel AS would take out the soul of that person in a very calm and peaceful way, that person would not even feel the pain of death but for this you have to be a believer. After the death of a person, he/she is buried in the graveyards where the real beginning starts. In the grave two angels will come and ask the person three questions. They will be: Who is your Lord? Who is your prophet? What is your religion? A believer who constantly kept remembering Allah will answer these questions very easily, but the Disbelievers will not be able to open their mouth.

The graves of a true believer will be very peaceful, but the graves of the Disbelievers will be a terrifying one, it will be filled with scorpions, snakes, etc. There will be torment for the people who disbelieved. The graves of Disbelievers would be very dark and filled with insects and reptiles. The graves of the Disbelievers would contract, and it will contract to an extent that the ribs of the person will combine in each other and shatter, the grave will relax and then contract again in the same manner. The graves of the believers would be filled with Noor and there would be protection for them of everything. The graves of believers would be peaceful and fragrant, and they would be able to answer the questions of Munkar and Nakir (Angels of Grave) with ease.

Now regarding this our prophet has mentioned a way to be protected from the torment of the grave. The prophet Muhammad (ﷺ) said that the person who recites Surah Mulk every night then that person would be protected from the torment of the grave. Also, you should visit graveyards as they will remind you of your final destination. No matter how much you earn in your life, no matter how much good relationships you have, no matter how big your house is, no matter where you live in the end it will be only a piece of land and you, no money or friend would be there to help you only your deeds will be there. In the end you will be mixed in the soil, and no one will remember you after a few days. No one will be there for you anymore, no one will be there waiting for you. *It will be only you and Allah there.*

Allah Created everything in a pair
as he created Death and Birth
No one has immorality, beware
whoever lives and lived on earth

wherever you may be, death will overcome
whether it be fortified tower or a slum
Death will come to you, none can run away
What Allah has ordained, one can't delay

It is Allah Who calls back your soul
upon your death and when you sleep
Allah is the one to be extol
and the one Who is in control

Allah is the most just full and the best of planner
Both good and evil won't die in a same manner
the good one will die with ease
and the evil with tormenting breeze

Life of this world is no more than a delusion of
enjoyment

(Quran 3:185)

XI

DAY OF JUDGMENT

Guard yourself against the day on which no soul will be of help to another. No intercession....

(Quran 2:48)

We have mentioned the day of judgment in many previous chapters. But what exactly is the day of judgment? What will happen on that day? Let us know about it in detail and know why we fear it.

The day of judgment will be the ending of something as well as starting of some other thing. What exactly? It will be the end of the world and the beginning of eternity. It will be the day on which every person who was born from the People of Adam AS to the People of Prophet Muhammad(ﷺ) will be raised again for their judgment. It will be the day on which Allah will be in full anger. No one will be protected from Allah's wrath except the righteous ones. Everyone would be feared on the day of judgment, no one will recognize each other, even your father or mother or brother or sister or spouse will recognize you. The best friends will be the greatest enemies of each other except for those who were righteous and guided each other to the path of Allah.

Allah will say to his feared people that why are you feared, feared should be those who did wrong you were my righteous slave there is no need for you to fear. It will be the day on which every deed, bad or good, of the person would be calculated and that person would be accountable for the things he did during his lifetime. Where Did he spend his youth? How did he spend it? Even your body parts will give accounts of what you made them do. Whether you used them in good things or used them in evil. Everything would be counted whether it be as small as the particle of sand.

Nothing would be left. It is on you how you spend your life but remember there is a day on which you have to face The Almighty, The All knower. Not even a single person will be left, everyone would have to give their accounts. And there will not be any oppression as small as the grain of sand, it will depend all on your deeds. Your deeds decide your eternity, your faith decides your eternity. It is on you how you shape your eternity. It is on you whether you want to be safeguarded by Allah Almighty on that day or face Allah's wrath. And trust me there is no one who wants to face the anger of God. The day of judgment is real, and it will occur and to believe in this day is a part of Tawheed. And whoever denies it has not yet fully understood the concept of Tawheed.

There will be no escaping from that day whether you are going to Jannah or Jahannam, every soul will face that day.

Let us understand what exactly will happen there according to the Quran and Hadith. There will be many signs before the day of judgment and the last of them will be the blowing of the trumpet by Angel Israfeel AS. After that every person to ever live on this world will be resurrected, from the people of Adam to the people' of Muhammad (ﷺ).

Every person will gather at a single place known as Hashr. It is the place where the judgment would be given. The place where you would've to give your all accounts whether they are good or bad. There will be three groups of people, The Idolaters, the people of the Books like Jews and Christians and then there will be Muslims. Firstly, without any questioning the Idolaters would be thrown into the hellfire with their idols and the idols will work as the fuel of the fire. Then the Jews and Christian will be asked why you got deviated from the right path, the Christians will say that they were told that Isa AS is the son of God,

Then Allah will bring Isa ibn maryam and ask him did you told them that you are the son of God he will say, no I didn't tell them that, instead I told them to worship the only God the almighty Allah. Then the Christians will be thrown in the hellfire. After this the same thing will happen to the Jews and they will also be thrown in the hellfire likewise. After this there will be the questioning of the Muslims, Every Muslim will give his accounts to Allah and on that basis, they will be sent towards hell and paradise.

The people would have to pass a bridge known as the Sirat which is as thin as a hair and as sharp as a sword. The righteous would cross it at the speed of light, some will pass it running, some will by walking, some by crawling and some will fall from it and reach hell. The people who will pass the Sirat then go to another bridge known as the Qantara where they would resolve their personal issues with their relatives after that the soul would become pure and they would enter Paradise the eternal home of a believer.

*Be mindful of it. When to God we all will return
And every soul will be paid for what it has done
when justice will be served
And reward for those who deserve*

*When the sun & moon will set together
And the river will be set to fire
The close ones will leave one another
The transgressors won't be able to
conspire*

*When the faces of righteous will be bright
And wicked one will be turned dusty
The Pregnant will delivers premature
The Nursing Women will leave their kids thirsty*

*It is the day when everyone will scare to death
Except those who God Wills to leave
The deniers will cry out loud instead
happy will be those who used to believe*

It will be day of terror for the guilty and the day of
justice for the innocent

UNIT VII: After Life

As stated in unit IV description, there are two different destinations, one which is hell another which is heaven, and each destination has a different route.

The route to HELL is easier

It is easier because he/she can achieve the destination by anger, Sins, Nafs (desires) doing everything bad one knows and doing it without regret. Using tongue to curse or not using to speak good, eyes to watch what is forbidden, using hand and legs to get closer to it and letting the desire to win to earn the olive-sized pleasure and gaining the anger of ALLAH

The route to HEAVEN is quite opposite

It is because the Satan whispers in your ears to make you astray from Allah like he is. The route is not easy as the surroundings and environment provokes you to do it by saying everyone is enjoying this worldly life, why don't you? It is your desire that you created it to do what is prohibited. One simple way, one may achieve Jannah (Heaven) is to do good and to be good.

The route to Hell is full of flowers (Desires) which gives you pleasure
when you break the flower or smell it but in the end, it always decays
And the route of heaven has different places to visit.
So, visit them like a traveller and enjoy the utmost. (what's permissible)

XII

HELL

Allah Huma Ajirni Minan Naar
(Oh, Allah protect me from the hellfire)

"May Allah protect us from it". You may have heard people saying this very often, but they don't do anything to be protected from it. This shows how much people fear it, how much they want to be protected by it, maybe they are not praying but they fear "Hell". And on the other hand, some people offer salah and also fear hell. But the important thing that the people don't understand is that offering Salah only can't protect you from hell, yet it is the most crucial thing to be protected but one has to do other things beside Salah, they have to restrain themselves from the Major Sins, they have to restrain themselves from doing what is evil or supporting what is evil. They have to restrain from oppressing the weak.

Now, for example, A person offers Salah, but he believes in astrology or believes that someone other than Allah could help him/her (which is shirk), then do you think that that person could enter Jannah? It is not possible, why? We will explain it in further chapter (Major Sins).

Before moving forward, let us take a glance at how terrifying Hell will be. Hell is indeed terrifying and there is nothing as horrifying or terrifying as Hell, that is the reason people want to be protected from it. Hell will be full of fire, everywhere there will be fire, people will be burning in that fire for eternity, just imagine burning in the fire till eternity. You and I can't put our hands over a candle for a few seconds, then imagine what will be the situation in hell, the whole body will be burning for endless time. People would be used as fuel for the fire of Hell. There would be no one to save you from the wrath of Allah.

The main thing is who would be in Hell. Who will be the unlucky ones? Will they be the people who didn't pray? Will they be the ones who disobeyed their parents? Will they be the ones who were arrogant? Will they be the one who said bad things about others on their backs? Will they be the one who did Zina? Will they be the one who used to take Riba? Will they be the one who were not kind to others? Of course, these are the people who would be in the hell fire, of course they will be the ones from which the Hell would be filled. Of course, they will be the ones who will taste the torment for the endless time. These will be the people who were completely distracted by the lust of the world and went astray, these will be the people who forgot the Akhirah for their Duniya. As a result, they will taste the exchange of that worldly life. They will be there for eternity. Also, the Munafiqs will be in Hell as well, now what is a Munafiq? A Munafiq (hypocrite) is a person who claims to be a Muslim in front of others but is not actually a Muslim, they say good things about people on their faces but bad on their backs.

Prophet SAW said that these are the indications of a Munafiq (hypocrite): (i) Whenever he speaks, he lies. (ii) whenever he promises, he breaks it. (iii)Whenever he is trusted, he betrays **(Sahih Bukhari 33).** It is mentioned in the Quran that the

Munafiqs (hypocrites) will be in the lowest depths of the Fire and there would be no helper for them unless except those who repent, mend their ways, hold fast to Allah, and are sincere in their devotion to Allah; they will be with the believers. And Allah will grant the believers a great reward **(Quran 4:145-146).**

Now let us talk about the Justice of Allah. Allah's justice for the criminal is far better than the justice of the world. Let us know about this from this, suppose a person committed a hundred murders, will the justice of the world be able to kill the same man a hundred times? No, they will not, they can only hang or kill a person a single time and if a person committed a single murder, then also the person would be killed only a single time. Do you think this is justice? The punishment of Allah will be continuous for the wrongdoers. But on the other hand, if a person murdered someone and then repented to Allah sincerely then he might not go to Hell, but he would have to give the accounts of the murdered person. Which will be the perfect justice for a person so far. Indeed, Hell is terrifying, and we should fear it but only fear from Hell would not protect us from it.

Oh, the Mankind
 for Miserable, and the transgressors.
The Garment of Fire is for them.
the boiling water over their heads will be poured.
which will burn the bellies and skin.
and then again n again they will be restored

Oh, the Mankind
For Tyrant, and the Oppressors
An oozing pus they will be forced to drink
and from tree of the hell will be forced to eat
they'll try to escape but won't be able to
they'll be reconstructed but the torment will
continue

Oh, the Mankind
For wrongdoers, and the residents of hell
They won't be able to live nor to die
even the death is around, and they are in mid
and will blame each other for what they did
the followers and the wicked on whom they used to
rely

XIII

PARADISE

"May God make every one of us to enter paradise". "May God make us so good that we are able to enter it". You may have heard these words from many people around you. Everyone wants to go there but they don't want to prepare for it, they don't want to leave evil for it, they don't want to do good to enter it. What is that thing every person wants but doesn't do anything for it? Indeed, it is the beautiful Jannah (Paradise). It is Jannah that everyone wants, apart from Muslims, Non-Muslims also have the concept of Paradise. Now you can think how good Jannah would be, people from every religion have concepts of paradise. What is so good about Jannah that everyone wants it? What is Jannah? How is Jannah? Let's know about Jannah according to Islam.

Do you understand the meaning of perfect? Do you know how perfect looks? Can you imagine how a perfect thing looks? If yes! then you have known a small fraction of Jannah. By this I mean that Jannah will be far beyond our imagination. Jannah will be a completely, one hundred percent perfect place. Even by the description of Jannah in the Quran and Hadith, our human minds will not be able to perceive how good the Jannah will be. It will be a completely different realm, it is unmatched, even our fantasies could not go any near to how Jannah will be. This is the good about Jannah that every person wants, this is why Jannah is willed by many, even those who are not doing good in life.

How will be the Jannah? What will be there? How will it look? What will the people be like? Let us know the answers to these questions. The people of Jannah will meet all the prophets including Prophet Muhammad (ﷺ). In Jannah there will be gardens with rivers flowing beneath and there will be mansions for the people of Jannah. There will be no ill speech nor any hatred, everyone will live in peace. There will be no sorrow or grief. There will be eternal peace in Jannah. The righteous members of a family will reunite (Father, Mother, children, wife, siblings). There will be thrones for people and cushions set in a row. There will be rivers of water, milk and wine. There will be fruits that we would have eaten in this Duniya, but their taste will be lot better. Everyone would be of the same age; they will never get old. No one will die in Jannah. There will be angels who will greet the people of Jannah. Indeed, it will be the eternal home of the righteous and the pious.

Now, let's talk about the sad thing. We will now know who the people are, who will not be able to enter Jannah. Surely, they would be there because of their deeds. First of the people who would not be able to enter Jannah are the non-believers, they will be the one who didn't believe in the oneness of Allah, they will be those who rejected the guidance that was sent to them in the form of Prophets, Messengers, scriptures and even the people who lived amongst them and constantly kept reminding them of the right path but they didn't believe them and chose the wrong path. They will be there because of Shirk. For example: idol worshippers. Shirk is the biggest issue that stops a person from entering Jannah and enters you into hell. Apart from them many Muslims would also not be able to enter Jannah. A person who does not offer Salah at all, might not enter Jannah because Salah is the first thing about which a Muslim would be asked on the day of judgment. People who disobey their parents and misbehave with their parents Will be among the losers and they might not be able to enter Jannah. In the Quran it is mentioned that after the Haq of Allah there is the Haq of Parents. Obeying your parents is not only an Islamic teaching but it is our moral duty to obey our parents. So, the person who doesn't obey his/her parent might not be able to enter Jannah. Now there are people who are arrogant, they think of others as weak, they live in their own world of arrogance. Allah doesn't like arrogance at all. It is mentioned in **Surah Nisa, verse 173** that the people who are arrogant, Allah will punish them with serious punishment. So arrogant people are also the ones who might not go to Jannah. Similarly, Oppressors and Tyrants will also not be able to enter Jannah. There are several other types of people who might not go to Jannah. They are the ones who did Major Sins like Zina, Murder, Suicide, Fleeing from Battlefield, Black Magic, Riba (Interest), taking of an orphan's property, etc. These are the people who did not repent at all and kept doing the same thing over and over.

Apart from them, the completely opposite of these types of people, are the ones who would go to Jannah without any problem. They will be the one who didn't disobey their parents, they didn't do Zina, murder, Suicide, they stayed away from Riba, they thought good of people, treated everyone with equality and kindness, treat the poor with respect and didn't regard to them as weak, etc. They will be the people who might go to Jannah, and they will stay there forever. Allah will pay them for their kindness and put them in his gardens under which the river flows.

Oh, The Mankind
For good doers, and the virtuous
Paradise is for them as vast as heavens and earth
and cloth of pure silk & rich brocade for them to wear
this is what Allah promised to the creation
For the one who used to sacrifice and fear

Oh, The Mankind
For humble, and the righteous
They will provide with pure spouses
and ALLAH's provision will never end
there will be maiden with gorgeous eyes
A life with no death they can't comprehend

Oh, The Mankind
For faithful, and those who obeyed
They'll be in garden of bliss and on jeweled thrones
and have canopied couches with extended shade
They'll have rivers of water milk honey & wine
for the ones who were patient & Prayed

Oh, The Mankind
For humble, and who were foremost in faith
residents of paradise will be neither ill
nor destitute and they will be young forever[1]
they'll get whatever they will
A beauty than a human mind can't endeavor

then which of your Lord's favor you will you both deny

(Quran 55: 49)

***Reference.**

1)Abu Huraira reported Allah's Apostle (may peace be upon him) as saying: He who would get into Paradise (would be made to enjoy such an everlasting) bliss that he would neither become destitute, nor would his clothes wear out, nor his youth would decline. (Sahih Muslim Book 40, Number 6802)

UNIT VIII: Mercy On the Repentant

Greatest Mercy can only be done by the one who has the greatest power to make anyone suffer; this is what mercy means to its greatest realm.

"Allah created a hundred mercies, and He placed one mercy among his creation, they show mercy to one another by it, and there are ninety-nine mercies with Allah." Jami` at-Tirmidhi 3541

The one who creates something Has also the power to easily destroy it.
The one who created the torment can only be the most merciful.

XIV

MAJOR SINS

Allah Says, "O son of Adam, if your sins were to reach the clouds of the sky, then you were to ask Me to forgive you, I would forgive you and I would not mind."

(Sahih At Tirmidhi 3540)

In Islam there are two types of sins:

1. **Major Sins (Al-Kabirah)**
2. **Minor Sins (Al-Sagirah)**

Minor Sins or Al-Sagirah are those which are prohibited in Islam and can be forgiven by performing good deeds such as performing wudu or giving charity. These sins are normal, and people commit them without even realizing that they are doing sin. This includes sins such as Cursing, Bullying, imitating others clothing or lifestyle, not being helpful (sometimes), etc. Major sins or Al-Kabirah are those which are strictly prohibited in Islam and have severe punishments for them. These sins can only be forgiven by repentance and restraining from doing them again. These sins can be found very prominently in today's world. We are surrounded with these types of sins from everywhere. This includes Shirk, Murder, Taking of Riba, Zina, Taking over someone else's property, Black Magic, etc.

In this chapter we are going to talk about some of the major Sins in Islam.

Different Hadith mentions different numbers of Major Sins (Al-Kabirah). But here we are going to talk about only some of the Major Sins in Islam. Going forward with it, they are:

SHIRK: Shirk is the biggest Sins amongst all the Major Sins. It means to associate partners with Allah. It involves worshiping deities, gods, or anything other than Allah. This completely denies the belief in La Ilaha Ill allah (There is no God to be worshiped except Allah). Associating someone with Allah. is completely intolerable. The person who dies in the state of shirk will not be able to enter paradise at all. It is mentioned in The Qur'an that the people who worship their idols will become fuel for the hellfire on the day of judgment **(Qur'an 21:98).** But as we know that Allah forgives everyone, and he loves to forgive the people seeking forgiveness from him. The only way to be forgiven for shirk is to repent by heart. The person should not associate any partners with Allah from then on. Remember Allah loves those who repent, and the Paradise would be filled with the people who repented.

MURDER: If a person kills a believer deliberately then, this is also one of the greatest sins in Islam. By committing murder, you are not only ending the life of a person but also you are preparing a place in the hellfire for yourself. Allah. mentions in The Qur'an, "..... whoever takes a life—unless as a punishment for murder or mischief in the land—it will be as if they killed all of humanity and whoever saves a life, it will be as if they saved all of humanity....."**(Quran 5:32).** As per sharia, If the murderer repents sincerely then Allah shall forgive him of his sin. As the victim is not alive, there is no right for him in this life. But on the hereafter (Day of judgment), The murderer will have to answer on the victim's account. But if the murderer's repentance is correct and accepted by Allah., then the murderer would be made to compensate the victim until he is satisfied (in the hereafter). Now apart from hereafter, the person has to face the victim's next to kin in this Dunya. The sharia gives the next of kin three options, قصاص [Qisas (Eye for an eye)], ديات [Dabaat(Financial Compensation)] and forgiveness . It depends on the family or close relative of the victim whether they want قصاص (Here, to have the murderer killed) or ديات or they want to forgive the murderer. Remember Allah loves those who forgive others **(Qur'an 64:14).**

BLACK MAGIC: Black Magic started to practice from the era of Prophet Suleiman P.B.U.H(Solomon).   In The Qur'an it is mentioned that Solomon was not the one who disbelieved, it was the devils who disbelieved. The two angels Harût and Marût were the ones who taught people magic. They were a test of Allah for the people of that time, and hence they didn't teach anyone magic until they (Harût and Marût) say, "We are a trial, so don't disbelieve (by practicing magic)." **(Qur'an 2:102).** Black Magic is one of the biggest sin a person could perform. The person who practices magic will have to face a great torment in the hereafter, and that person has sold himself to the devils for this Duniya. But as we know that Allah. forgives those who repent sincerely, so if you are really guilty for what you have done, you are ready to leave every wrong thing for the sake of The Almighty then ask the person (on whom you practiced magic) to forgive you and then repent to Allah. sincerely with pure intentions. Surely Allah will accept your repentance if it is sincere. Indeed, Allah is the All forgiver and the best of planners. Remember, "Every son of Adam sins, and the best of the sinners are the repentant." **(Jami-at-Tirmidhi 2499)**

RIBA: Now, the most important of all the major sins, by which we are surrounded from all sides in the form of mortgages or other things, is Riba, or we can say interest. It is haram to give Riba (loan) or take Riba (interest on deposit). It has a reason for being haram, it is haram because Riba makes the poor poorer and the rich richer, Banks take money from the poor in the form of loans and give it to the rich in the form of interest. It is one of the most important things to be careful about in this era as most of the things are directly or directly connected to

Riba or Interest. Whether it is buying a land, buying a vehicle, buying a home or even depositing your money in the bank, it is all involving Riba in it because most of the banks and finance system are controlled by the top peoples who want to make the poor poorer and the rich rice richer. Now, I won't go deep in this matter because I am here to tell you about Riba from an Islamic point of view. It is mentioned in the Quran more than any other sin which itself tells us how big of a sin it is. It is the only sin against which Allah says that whoever doesn't restrain from taking Riba has started a war with Allah and his Messenger (ﷺ) **(Quran 2:279).** Just imagine a war, literally a war against the Almighty and his messenger(ﷺ). May Allah help us to stay away from Riba as much as possible.

ZINA: Zina is considered as one of major sins in Islam which is seeing one more after first glance intentionally, touching or even hanging out while enjoying with the na-mehram, the opposite gender to whom you are not married. It also means adultery, fortification etc. with whom you are not related. it is stated in the **(Quran 17:32)** that do not go near adultery .it is truly a shameful deed and an evil way.

Various Types of Zina Are: -
Zina through eyes: looking at unlawful things such as pornography and having multiple glances on opposite gender with lust also comes under this type of zina.
Zina through tongue: speaking of immoral things in a way which is prohibited which leads to **zina through hand** which means touching what is forbidden to touch for example shaking hands with the opposite gender
 Zina through ears: listening the talk of adultery
 Zina a Major sin that leads to betrayal and destroys the faith in harmony which is essential to keep the family happy and it might look exciting but only leads to sadness and a sorrowful life .the easiest way to get forgiveness in Islam for the sin like

zina or any other is to remember **ALLAH Al GHAFOOR , The Forgiver** ask forgiveness from him and trying best no to do it again and the best way to prevent zina form happening is to keep yourself busy as much as you can . If you still think that Zina shouldn't be prohibited, would you be happy if your mother, daughter, sister and wife commit zina or someone commits with them?

"O son of Adam, were you to come to Me with sins nearly as great as the earth and were you then to face Me, ascribing no partner to Me, I would bring you forgiveness nearly as great as it."

(Hadith Qudsi 34: 40)

No matter how times you sinned
Ask for forgiveness……

Who associate Allah with others
In worship have gone far astray[1]
Do not even go near adultery
It is truly a shameful and an evil way[2]

Do not defraud nor spread corruption
Don't take a life of anyone or yours with intention[3]
Intoxicants, gambling[4] are Satan's games
Nor call each other with offensive nicknames

Don't be unjust nor charge interest

And pay the alm taxes if you're being blessed
Don't get involved in activity like magic
Nor runaway from battlefield unless it's strategic[5]

Who does more wrong than the one
who fabricates Lies against God or claims
The sinners who don't repent
Will be in hell of eternity flames

...... and Remember
Jannah is full of those who repent

Allah will forgive you if you repent before dying,

but the time of death always remains uncertain.

XV

ALLAH'S MERCY

"In the name of Allah— The most compassionate, most merciful. Praise be to Allah, the master of the entire Universe."

(Qur'an 1:1-2)

Everything comes to an end, but Allah's Mercy doesn't. His mercy and blessings are showered on a person without any pause. The Almighty takes the test of his people by giving them difficulties like a disease or natural disaster. Most of the people become very stressed due to this, but this is a wonderful way of Allah's mercy as he erases the bad deeds of a person for each suffering caused. And the people who overcome these tests are the real strong believers. As we all know, Allah. is the most merciful, as he also forgives those who have committed major sins if their (the one who committed sin) repentance is true. There are many stories in the hadith and Qur'an which gives us the idea of Mercy of the most merciful. Here, in the second last chapter of the book we are going to shower light about some incidents which are the perfect examples of Allah's Mercy.

It is mentioned in **Sunan Al Tirmidhi 3107** that, Angel Jibreel (Gabriel) said to Prophet Muhammad (ﷺ) that he was putting mud from the sea in Firaun's (Pharaoh) mouth when he (Pharaoh) started to say, " I believe that there is no God except Allah, One in who people of Israel believed, in the fear that Allah's mercy would reach to him and he would be forgiven.

Now some people will argue that repentance is by heart and not by speech. Yes, it is true, but Firawn (Pharaoh) tried to repent after he experienced the torment (Azab), that's the reason he might not be forgiven.

There is another story mentioned in **Sahih Bukhari, Volume 4, Book 56, Number 676** stating the forgiveness of a murderer. There was a man who heartlessly killed Ninety-Nine people. After doing all this, he felt very guilty and remorseful. He went to a knowledgeable man and told him about his past. He also told him that he wanted to repent and become a better person. He asked, "I wonder if Allah will pardon me?" The Knowledgeable man was not able to digest this and said, "You will not be pardoned." After hearing this, the murder said, "Then I may as well kill you, too." And he killed that man also. Then he again went to another scholar and told him about his past and said, "I wonder, whether Allah will pardon me if I repent?" The scholar was a true wise man. He replied, "Who stands between you and repentance?" And advised him to repent at once and never go back to bad deeds. The man said, go to a place where more righteous people live. The murderer repented and with regret and decided to move to a more righteous neighborhood. While moving to the new neighborhood, his time came, and he died. After his death the angels of mercy and the angels of punishment came to take him. The angel of mercy argued that "He willed to become more righteous and was going to have the company of righteous people, so he deserves mercy. "The angel of punishment argued back and said, "He spent all his life doing sins and he was amongst the wrongdoers, so he deserves punishment." To solve this problem Allah sent Angel Jibreel (Gabriel) as an arbiter to solve the dispute. After hearing to both the sides Angel Jibreel (Gabriel) said, "Measure the ground, if the spot where he dies is close to the good people, then he belongs to the Angel of mercy and if the spot where he died is close to wicked people, then he belongs to the Angel of Punishment." Both the distances were measured and as the murder just set off to go to the righteous neighborhood and his time came, he died close to the wicked people. But the murderer's repentance was true, so Allah moved the spot from where he died to just outside the righteous neighborhood. Hence, the murderer was handed over to the Angel of Mercy. This story is a perfect example of Allah's mercy and there are more such stories depicting his Mercy.

You sinned a lot with body, repent once with soul
Allah the most merciful shall forgive you for whole

No matter how big your sins are
Yet Allah's mercy oversize it
Ask for Allah's forgiveness and repent
Just don't try to recommit or publicize it[6]

You move one step towards Allah
He moves thousands towards you
Your bad deeds are being replaced
By the righteous one you do
Every son of Adam sins

And the best is those who atone[7]
Allah's mercy precedes his Anger
Is what written on Allah's Throne[8]

You sinned a lot with body, repent once with soul
Allah the most merciful shall forgive you for whole

My words have come to an end, but Allah's mercy
won't...

---

*Reference...

1)shirk
2)zina
3)murder or suicide
4)intoxicant, gambling
5)magic or fleeing away from battlefield
6)Hazrat Abu Huraira narrated I heard Allah's Messenger (صلى الله عليه وسلم) saying. "All the sins of my followers will be forgiven except those of the Mujahirin (those who commit asin openly or disclose their sins to the people). (sahih-al-bukhari 6069)
7)Hazrat Anas narrated that the Prophet SAW said, "Every son of Adam sins,and the best the sinners are the repentant." :(Jami'At-Trimidhi 2499)
8)Hazrat Abu Huraira narrated that, Prophet (صلى الله عليه وسلم) said when allah had finished his creation he wrote over his throne: "My mercy precedes me anger". (sahih-al-bukhari:7453)

UNIT IX: THOUGHTS?

What we see, what we learn and what we read gives us
KNOWLEDGE,
the ability to use the knowledge we gain is
WISDOM,
both combined may change a particular person way of
living or may give us an impulse to think which is termed
as
THOUGHTS.

XVI

Thoughts?

"The Messenger of Allah said: 'When Allah wills good for a person, He causes him to understand the religion.'"

(Sunan Ibn Majah 220)

The final chapter of the book **Thoughts?** summarizes the whole book in a poem giving an invitation to introspection on Islamic beliefs and its teachings throughout the book. Making us ponder upon in a questioning way giving us thoughts with a question mark.

Thoughts with a question mark indicate uncertainty, curiosity and show that the person is seeking answers. It portrays that something is left open for discussion, further exploration and possibilities.

Thoughts (?) could be as simple as what to do today and as complex as what life actually is, but here the thoughts are highlighted on Islam in the easiest manner of contemplation poem to ever be.

Q

Is Allah not worthy of worship
or not to give you ease in hardship
Is he not capable to be your companion
or is he not the king of dominion

There were previous scriptures sent before
and prophets were sent previous too
Would you then also like to be denialist
like the people of that time used too

Isn't his revelation[1] enough to guide
to teach humanity and what's right
To teach you how to reside
and what is most upright

Wasn't there any messenger[2] to warn you
neither his lessons that taught you
Aren't you aware the challenges he faced
wasn't he not the one that Allah graced

Remember his last sermon try to retrieve
doesn't it give you a relieve
Wasn't there any way to pray
then what made you to fall astray

Was not there any way to help the people in need
Aren't you aware of oppression and misdeed
Then what led you to move your eyes away
then what led to move your eyes away

Won't the death come to you
and does the judgement day was Untold
Doesn't it give you a clear cue
and make the information uphold

Don't you believe in heaven and hell
then what made you to repel
The Sins we did are forgivable
in all mercy of the universe, Allah's always excel

Does these thoughts give you a question mark
and what are your thoughts till now all about
Doesn't the information make any construe
that has been spread in the book throughout

?

***Reference...**

1)QURAN

2)Prophet Mohammed()

★★★

A) Common questions in and about Islam: -

What is ISLAM?

Islam is the religion of peace. It is doing Good and to be good, speak good and to provide the poor. It is a religion that doesn't end with an ism. It is perfect, not the one who practices it.

It consists of mandatory units such as: -

- Faith (shahada)
- Prayer
- Pilgrimage
- Fast in the month of Ramadan (can be kept afterwards under certain conditions)
- Alms Giving (zakat)

Not all these are mandatory for every Muslim except faith and prayer. That is salah. And this particular religion is composed of three major units which are Faith in Allah, Prophet Muhammad and the Quran. If you keep one aside it isn't complete.

What If Muslims are following the wrong religion and the other one is right?

To know the truth about the religion whether it is Islam, or any other is to study it. By self and by the book not by the media, Society, the act of humans belonging to the religion you want to know about, Judgment of others who hate it.

Guidance doesn't come from Allah until you humble yourself and try to get it. Society now is in intellectual laziness. Thinking about what will happen after you get knowledge of it and what

people will say. If you don't get to know the religion, how will you know the outcome? It is stated in the Qur'an:
Let there be no compulsion in religion, for the truth stands out clearly from falsehood. (Quran 2:256)

What is Jihad?

Jihaad linguistically means to struggle and technically to fight and struggle for the cause of Allah. however, jihad can be classified in various things That are: -

- Jihad is to fight against the devil
- Jihad is to fight against your own desires
- Jihad is to fight against the enemies of Islam
- Jihad is to fight against the hypocrites
- Jihad against the sinners

Jihaad doesn't Mean only to fight and kill it also means to resist and prevent, and it can also be done by words not only by attack. Prophet Muhammad PBUH always encouraged Jihad by words.

Major Jihad is to fight against self-desires and minor Jihad is to fight for self-defense. Jihad is to protect it is not to harm.

Why are only Muslims are called terrorists and does the Quran promote terrorism?

If we look upon the history, The killings of millions in Germany was done by the Hitler who isn't a Muslim, what happened to Nagasaki in Japan was done by America which isn't a Muslim country. There are too many other stories of mass murders and killings not done by a Muslim or a Muslim country. But they aren't called terrorists but why is that?

This is because of what the Western media shows the public by creating images Of Muslims in many movies by showing Muslims as terrorists and making the people believe that terrorist looks like the one who is wearing a turban or having a beard without a mustache. **In the Quran it states in chapter no. 5 verse 32 that whoever takes a life—unless as a punishment for murder or mischief in the land—it will be as if they killed all of humanity; and whoever saves a life, it will be as if they saved all of the humanity**
Islam is what is in the Quran not what a person with a name of Muslim does and not what the western society and media portrays.

What are the rights of non-Muslims in an Islamic state?

A non- in an Islamic state has all the right to practice his religion, right to have churches etc., Inheritance law, way of marriage etc. will be of their own and they have a free will to join the army. The rulership has the responsibility for the protection of non muslims.

Jizya tax: - Muslims having wealth over equivalent to 87.48 grams of gold and or 612.36 grams are required to pay 2.5% of their wealth each year to charity called zakat (Pillar of Islam which is mandatory to be performed) Same amount is to be paid by non

Muslims men who are free, able bodied, healthy, and of sound mind in an Islamic state in the form of Jizya tax. Poor people are not required to pay Jizya tax.

What is the Status of Women in Islam?

In Islam both female and male are equal before God in terms of receiving both equal rewards and accountability. The one thing that distinguishes people is their goodness. They have the right to inheritance, the right to equal pay, the right to choise of spouse (The prophet also asked for the approval of her daughter (Hazrat Fatima RA) for her marriage, the right to education and the right to divorce etc. But in some countries, they don't follow Islam they follow their cultural practices and traditions passed on by their ancestors. Prophet Muhammad SAW said to treat women nicely. In his last sermon he said treat your woman well and be kind to them. They are your committed partners and helpers. It was a woman (Hazrat Khadija RA, wife of the prophet) who helped the prophet to learn business. At the time of Marriage, the dowry called Mehr in Islam is to be given by the groom to the bride as a gift and security of the bride and the amount is decided by the bride and her guardian and it is mandatory. There is nothing to be given by the family of the bride. Similarly at time of inheritance the male has to distribute the property to his family what he has and the female is not obliged to give her part of the property .*Islam isn't the religion that oppresses women, it is the religion which uplifts them at the highest degree* .The messenger of Allah Said : *"The most complete of the believers in faith, is the one with the best character among them. And the best of you are those who are best to your women. "*Jami` at-Tirmidhi 1162.

What Is Sharia Law?

Sharia law is based on the Quran and the teachings of Prophet Muhammad SAW. Sharia (which means path) law mainly focuses on protecting five things which are religion, life, lineage, intellect and communal wealth. The law doesn't only punish, it gives you rights, justice, and prevents you from doing wrong like drinking alcohol and charging interest for the loan you provided. If The rules are strict then crime itself decreases. In an Islamic country sharia law isn't applicable on minorities in case of inheritance, marriage etc.

What is Polygamy in Islam?

Polygamy is a major point of dispute and is among the most important topics which needs to be clarified. In Islam it is not mandatory for a person to marry more than one woman, it is only permissible. A man can marry more than one woman if he wants but Allah says in the Qur'an that marry one or two or three or four only if you can be just with them all equally and if you can't be just with all of them then marry only one. If you look at it carefully then you will come to know that this law is helpful for women who are widows, orphans, etc. If a man marries a widow or an orphan, he can provide a shelter for her and provide her with her basic needs. Also, the wife of the Man has the right to make an agreement at the time of the marriage which prevents the husband to marry another woman without the consent and agreement of his wife.

B) Ending the debate on Prophet Muhammad (ﷺ) marriage with Aishah (ra) and his multiple marriages: -

Hazrat Aishah was the only virgin he married. As a woman she was the most learned in jurisprudence and knowledge. Coming to her age of marriage In Hadith **Sunan an-Nasa'i 3379** *It was narrated that 'Aishah said: "The Messenger of Allah married me when I was six and consummated the marriage with me when I was nine.* (Hadith is a talk which may be brief or elaborated." Technically Hadith means the narration of the sayings, doings or approvals (Taqrir) of Muhammad (peace be upon him)). From Hazrat Aishah herself we get to know the age of her marriage. During her teaching or while she was a military commander, she would have accused the prophet if he did anything wrong, but she didn't. 88 renowned scholars learnt from her, and she narrated over 2000 hadiths in which she never accused the prophet for anything. She had played an important role in the religion Islam. *If we look at the history Tipu sultan, Baldwin IV and Shivaji Maharaj all started their military Conquest below the age of 16 or at age 16, there many too who did it and some even conquered places. Could a boy at this age of current time even participate in war or even be mentally prepared for it? If he can, then Hazrat Aishah's marriage with the Prophet is Absolutely wrong.* In many major religions the age of marriage is considered the time after when the person hits puberty, not when they reach age 18 or 21 which is by law. Things were different as of now even the life expectancy was also different.

Now coming to the 2nd most highlighted topic against the prophet which is his **multiple marriages**. Many Islamophobes accused him of being the prophet and was lustful. Prophet Muhammad SAW's first marriage was with hazrat Khadija when he was twenty-five and she was at age forty. She passed away when she was sixty-five and the prophet was fifty. He didn't marry any other women until she died same scholars say he didn't marry to anyone even after two years of her death, would a lustful person do that, would a lustful person marry a women 15 year older than him and don't marry another woman during his youth when libido is found high in men?

Multiple marriages of his could be understood only with three main reasons. The first one is to build **alliances** and connections with other tribes and empires as no leader would attack a person to whom your daughter is married. Second is that during wars many died so many women become widows. During that time many companions married widowed women and the prophet too for the **protection of widowed women**. *Do you think a lustful person will marry a 50-year-old widow woman who already has five children?*

The last reason is **teaching and education. The** companions of the prophet told the hadith outside of the house but what about the hadith inside his household and some special situation of women who narrated them, the wives. Prophet Muhammad could not teach each nonrelated woman one by one so a private education system was built, and not all women could directly talk with the prophet for the same topics. Almost half of the Islamic rulings and teachings come from the wives of the prophets, Hazrat Aishah narrated more hadith than Hazrat Umar and Hazrat Abu Bakr combined. Although Islam limits the marriage to only four wives for us Was not put to him like the midnight prayer tahajjud was mandatory for him, but it is optional for us. The right to multiple marriages to him was mainly due to the last reason which is **teaching and education.** To teach women for special situations and fulfill this essential duty there have to be multiple wives who are different from one another in terms of *character, personality, areas of interest and age.* The limitation of four marriages was not put up to him but at the same time it added more responsibility of managing and treating more wives equally as treating the wives unjustly is disgraced in Islam and a noble with full of responsibilities and difficulties than any other human would never do that.

Search the truth from the Islamic books and the Quran not from the haters of Islam who will always try to deceive us.

C) Famous personalities about Islam and its messenger: -

Thomas Carlyle, a Scottish author and intellectual said the lines that have been said about Prophet Muhammad (ﷺ) by the west are shameful. *How one man on his own can unite warring times and wandering Bedouins and make them the most powerful and civilized nation in less than two decades*. A silent great soul. One of those who cannot bump Ernest, he wished to kindle the world because the creation of the world had ordered so. His readiness to undergo persecutions for his belief the high moral character of his companions who believed in him always looked up to him as a leader

Prince Bismark, Ottoman Bismark a Duke of Lauenburg, German statesman and Diplomat said O Muhammad (ﷺ), I am sad, for we are not contemporaneous! This book that you are both its teacher and spreader, is not your book since it is divine. Denying that it is divine is a ridiculous act, like nullifying well-known sciences. Because of this, humanity saw an outstanding power like you once but will never be able to see in the future. *I humbly bow to your esteemed character with the utmost degree.*

Mahatma Gandhi a nationalist and freedom fighter, said "I wanted to learn about the life of the person who without dispute ruled the hearts of millions of people. When I read it, I certainly believed that there was no role for the sword Keeping for Islam to make ground in those years.

Keeping himself in the background, he was true to his words, fair, selfless to his followers and companions, fearless and courageous. With His trust in God in the task he took on was certain and clean. There was no need to carry a sword to overcome any burden when you had these qualities...I was sad to see that there was nothing to read more about this incredible life after I finished reading the second volume of the book about him.

Michael H. Hart Author of famous book the 100: A Ranking of the Most Influential Persons in History said "My choice Of MUHAMMAD (ﷺ) To lead, the list of the World's most influential people may surprise some readers and may be questioned by others, but he was the only man in history who was supremely successful on both the religious and secular level. "Humanity has never experienced a more perfect religion than Islam from the aspects of ethics, philosophy, and law. *I believe there will never be a person as perfect as Muhammad* (ﷺ) *with every aspect of his existence.*

George Bernard Shaw, an Irish author and writer, winner of the 1925 Nobel Prize in literature said, i have studied him. The wonderful man. And in my opinion far from being an anti-Christ, he must be called the Savior of Humanity. *I believe that if a man like him were to assume the dictatorship of the modern world, he will succeed in solving its problems in a way that would bring it much-needed peace and happiness.* I have prophesied about the faith of Muhammad (ﷺ) that it would be acceptable to the

Europe of tomorrow as it is beginning to be acceptable to the Europe of today.

Karen Armstrong a British author, and scholar of the history of religions said Muhammad's () command on hijab for women is a protocol not to humiliate but to elevate them. His stand was against the imperialists of the west. *He aimed and achieved to fix not only for his society but the whole history of humankind from corruption and establish a just society.* He was very merciful towards children, and children loved him very much in return. Every time he returned to the city, children would hug him lovingly. *He was an intelligent and charismatic leader who changed the course of history.*

★★★

D) Some lessons from the Quran: -

Towards Parents

The Quran says to be kind towards parents, honor them and be humble with them. If one or both reach old age in your care, never say them even 'ugh', nor yell at them. Rather address them respectfully and pray for them *O* Allah*! Be merciful to them as they raised me when I was young.*

Towards non-Muslims

The Quran says that Allah does not forbid anyone from dealing kindly and fairly with those who have neither fought nor driven you out of your homes. Surely God loves those who are fair.

Towards Decency

The Quran says to the believing men to lower the gaze and guides their chastity and believing women to lower their gaze and guides their chastity. And to draw veils over their chests, not revealing the adornments (hair, arms, legs and body shape) except what normally appears.

Towards Humility

The Quran says to not walk on earth arrogantly and pridefully, surely you can neither crack the earth nor stretch to the height of the mountains. Don't turn your nose up to people. Be moderate in your pace and lower your voice, for the ugliest of all voices is certainly the braying of donkeys. Surely God does not like whoever is arrogant and boastful.

Towards Social Etiquette

The Quran says if an evildoer brings any news, verify it so you do not harm people unknowingly, becoming regretful for what you have done. Do not let anyone ridicule others; they may be better than them. Do not defame each other nor call each other by offensive nicknames and avoid suspicious for indeed suspicious are sinful, do not spy, nor backbite one another. There is no good in secret talks-except those encouraging charity, kindness, reconciliation between people, goodness and righteousness.

E) 99 Names of Allah: -

Allah is the most or entirely merciful , THE BESTOWER OF MERCY , the king and the owner of dominion , the absolutely pure , the **perfection and giver of peace** , the one who gives emaan and security , **the guardian/the witness/the overseer** , the all mighty , the compeller/restorer , the supreme/majestic , the creator/maker, the originator , the all and oft forgiving , **the fashioner** , the subduer/the ever dominating , *the giver of gifts* , the provider , the all-knowing/the omniscient , the withholder , the extender , the ruducer/abaser , *the exalter/the elevator* , the dishonourer/the humiliator , the all hearing , the all-seeing , the judge/the giver of justice , the utterly just , the subtle one/the most gentle , the most forbearing , the magnificent/the supreme , THE FORGIVING/ THE EXCEEDINGLY FORGIVING , the most heigh/the exalted , the greatest/the most grand , the preserver/the heedful/ all protecting , **the sustainer** , the majestic/most generous/the most esteemed , **the watchful** , the responsive one , the all-encompassing/the boundless , the all wise , the most loving , the glorious/the most honorable , **the resurrection/the raiser of the dead** , the all and ever witnessing , *the absolute truth* , the trustee/the disposer of affairs , the all strong , the firm/the steadfast , the protecting associate , **the praiseworthy** , the all enumerating/the counter , *the initiator* , the restorer/therein stator , the giver of life , the bringer of death/the destroyer , the ever-living , the sustainer/the self-subsisting , the perceiver , the illustrious/the magnificent , THE ONE , the unique/the only one , the eternal/satisfier of needs , the capable , the powerful , the omnipotent , the expediter/the promoter , the delayer/the retarder , the first , the last , the manifest , **the knower of hidden** , the governor/the patron , *the self-exalted* , the source of goodness/the kind benefactor , the ever pardoning/the relenting , the avenger , the pardoner , the most kind , the master of kingdom , *the possessor of glory and honor/lord of majesty and generosity* , the equitable , the gatherer/the unitor, the self-sufficient/the wealthy , the enricher , the withholder , THE DISTRESSOR , the propitious , the light/the illuminator , the guide , the incomparable originator , the ever-surviving/the everlasting , the inheritor/the heir , the infallible teacher , **the forbearing/the patient** .

*DID HE NOT FIND YOU
UNGUIDED THEN GUIDED
YOU?*

[Quran 93: 7]

One needs to make following declaration, In Order if he/she wants to become Muslim:

Ash-hadu alla ilaha illa Allah, wa ash-hadu anna Muḥammadan rasûlu Allah

I bear witness that there is no god worthy of worship except God, and I bear witness that Muhammad is the Messenger of God.

Religion is perfect, not the one who Practices it, by studying the book rather than the appearance of any human being. it will make you more clear about it. We aren't talking only about the book we wrote, but the other book of our religion either written or translated too.

Some book we recommend are:

- The Clear Quran: A Thematic English Translation of the Message of the Final Revelation by Dr. Mustafa Khattab
- The sealed nectar (Ar-Raheeq Al-Makhtum) by Safiur Rahman Mubarakpuri (biography of Prophet Mohammed 
- Islam: Beliefs and Teachings by Ghulam Sarwar

★★★

Thanking You Readers

The book has come to an end but for any feedback, further query and question mail us at: -

allaboutislam.queries@gmail.com

Your feedback means a lot to us

~Arham and Areeb